# Abortion in Context:
## A Select Bibliography

compiled by
### Charles Dollen

# The Scarecrow Press, Inc.
# Metuchen, N. J.     1970

# Contents

## Introduction

The pill, the atom and the gene were the tremendous
trifles that exercised mankind during 1969. It was Herb
Caen who pointed out that human sexuality, world peace and
racism, along with inflation and environment, were the major
issues that affected the new priorities of human values.
These will be reflected throughout our culture in the 1970's.

Abortion was, perhaps, one of the most emotional
issues and it received major attention from a wide range of
authors and journals. It will continue to be news for a long
time to come and the resolution of this conflict will have a
major impact on the value placed on human life.

I started compiling this bibliography as a favor for
my colleague and class-mate, Dr. William Shipley, Chair-
man of the University of San Diego Philosophy Dept. It was
intended to support his fascinating research into the whole
area of abortion. This compilation lists books and articles
in the English language that are reasonably available to
American scholars and libraries. The emphasis is on ma-
terials that may be described as "recent" at the time of
publication, with emphasis on the years 1967-1969. However,
some older but still valuable material has been listed, such
as the Eugene Quay material with its truly remarkable
bibliography.

What started out as a simple bibliography on abortion
soon broadened out into the contextual setting of the subject.
"Text without context is pretext," writes St. Augustine and

as I discovered how many learned and popular disciplines were interested in abortion, it became evident that I would have to indicate the whole field. This includes marriage, family, contraception, the sexual revolution and the very vocal opposition. The question of exactly when life begins is as burning an issue today as it was in the time of Aquinas. Are oral contraceptives and intra-uterine devices really abortifacients and, for that matter, is abortion properly to be considered contraception?

Leaving to Dr. Shipley and his peers the answers to some of these vexing questions, Abortion in Context offers a generous selection of the material in which the main theme, the cultural and philosophical aspects of abortion, should be studied. A source index is included since the experience of many years at a library reference desk has taught that scholars frequently remember a publisher or a magazine name when they have forgotten the author or title.

Two interests parallel the abortion debate. The population question and the legalization of homosexuality keep crossing into this literature. The fight to allow "consenting adults" to have full sexual freedom, in private, follows exactly the paths that were trod by those wishing to legalize abortion. The arguments between those who claim the world is over-populated and those who deny it frequently stumble over the idea that abortion is one answer to over-population, poverty and social welfare programs.

A surprising development is the realization that Catholic-Protestant unity may well run afoul of the sexual revolution. Differing viewpoints on abortion, birth control, divorce and re-marriage may prove insurmountable. This theological and philosophical debate is also chronicled in this bibliography. Both sides are voluble in presenting their propositions and we can only hope that in the multitude of words, someone will discover acceptable compromises.

\* \* \* \* \*

It is always a pleasure to say a word of thanks to the many people who helped with advice, encouragement and typing. My thanks are extended to Mr. B. Gene Hunt, assistant librarian, who arranged for me to have the time available. Then to Mrs. Ellen Curzon, the ever-efficient and cheerful secretary; Sr. Clare Louise Chandler, reference librarian at the University of San Diego; Mrs. Vera Hrusoff, Head of the library's technical services, and Fr. Joseph McDonnell of the U. S. D. Religious Studies department. Lila Everson, Vera Stern, Lawander Bernabe and Terry Mignogna of the library staff kept a sharp eye out for the very latest material to come into the building and rushed it to my desk. Even the student assistants became interested and the young men at the circulation desk, Rich Picard and Tony McElroy, started saving information for me. Finally, I want to thank Miss Irene Gutierrez, a neighboring librarian for San Diego schools, who was most helpful, and Fr. Paul Goda, S. J., of the University of Santa Clara, who sent helpful items.

If it were customary to dedicate bibliographies, this one would be dedicated to the memory of the late W. Roy Holleman, Librarian of the San Diego College for Women, who died suddenly in late 1969. His career in professional librarianship covered more years than I have lived and he was an example of all that is fine in librarians.

# ABORTION IN CONTEXT

## Main Entries by Both Author and Title

Aarons, Z. Therapeutic abortion and the psychiatrist, American Journal of Psychiatry 124: 745-747, 1967.                                                   A-1

Abandoned Spouse. Montserrat-Torrents, Jose, Bruce, 1969.                                               A-2

Abels, S. First year of the abortion act, Lancet 1: 1051-1052, May 24, 1969.                               A-3

Aborted discussion. Ave Maria 103: 17, Feb. 5, 1966.                                                      A-4

Abortion. Gough, C. Modern Churchman 10: 231-235, Apr. 1967.                                          A-5

Abortion. Harrington, Paul, Linacre Quarterly, 1969 issues.                                              A-6

Abortion. Hayes, Thomas, Commonweal 85: 676-679, Mar. 17, 1967.                                       A-7

Abortion. Hentoff, Margot, Jubilee 14: 4-5, Apr. 1967.                                                   A-8

Abortion. Lader, Lawrence, Bobbs-Merrill, 1966.       A-9

Abortion. Lewit, Sarah, Scientific American 220: 21-27, Jan. 1969.                                       A-10

Abortion. Notre Dame Law Review 43: 686-690, June 1968.                                               A-11

Abortion. O'Donnell, Thomas, Linacre Quarterly 34: 364-366, Nov. 1967.                                  A-12

Abortion. Ransil, Bernard, Paulist Press, 1969.        A-13

Abortion. St. John-Stevas, Norman, Tablet 223: 662-664, July 5, 1969.                                   A-14

Abortion. Schur, Edwin, Annals of the American
    Academy of Political and Social Science 376:
    136-147, Mar. 1968.                   A-15

Abortion. Simms, Madeline, Twentieth Century
    175:#1032, 1967.                       A-16

Abortion. Tietze, Christopher, Scientific American
    220:21-27, Jan. 1969.                A-17

Abortion: a fetal viewpoint. Romanowski, Richard,
    Linacre Quarterly 34:276-281, Aug. 1967.    A-18

Abortion: a Jewish view. Klein, Isaac, Dublin
    Review 241:382-390, Winter 1967.         A-19

Abortion à la suisse. Marr, Susan, New Statesman
    73: Apr. 7, 1967.                     A-20

Abortion: a legal view. Byrn, Robert, Commonweal
    85:679-680, Mar. 17, 1967.           A-21

Abortion: a painful lesson for Britain. Time
    93:48, Mar. 7, 1969.                  A-22

Abortion, a symposium. Commonweal June 30, 1967.   A-23

Abortion act in practice. Richard, E., British
    Medical Journal 1:778, Mar. 22, 1969.     A-24

Abortion Act 1967. Flood, Peter, Clergy Review
    53:42-48, Jan. 1968.                 A-25

Abortion act, 1967. Samuels, Alec, Medicine,
    Science and the Law 9:3-11. Jan. 1969.    A-26

Abortion: an Ethical Discussion. Church information
    Office, Westminster, 1965.             A-27

Abortion and dialogue. Commonweal 85:667-668,
    Mar. 17, 1967.                     A-28

Abortion and divorce reform. America 116:200,
    Feb. 11, 1967.                     A-29

Abortion and guffaws for chastity. Brown, J., New
    England Journal of Medicine 281:276-278, July
    31, 1969.                        A-30

Abortion and mental health.  *America* 116:239,  Feb.
   18,  1967.                                                          A-31
Abortion and pluralism.  *Commonweal* 85:582-583,
   Feb. 24,  1967.                                                     A-32
Abortion and promise-keeping.  Green, Ronald,
   *Christianity and Crisis* 27:109-113,  May 15,
   1967; 195-196, Aug. 7; 220-222, Oct. 2, 1967.      A-33
*Abortion and Public Policy*.  Shaw, Russell, Family
   Life Bureau, N. C. W. C. ,  1968.                               A-34
Abortion and the Catholic Church.  Noonan, John,
   *Natural Law Forum* 12:85-131,  1967.                      A-35
Abortion and the Catholic faith.  Grisez, Germain,
   *American Ecclesiastical Review* 159:96-115,
   Aug. 1968.                                                           A-36
Abortion and the crime-sin spectrum.  Lorenson,
   Willard, *West Virginia Law Review* 70:20-25,
   Dec. 1967.                                                           A-37
Abortion and the law.  McLaughlin, John, *St.*
   *Anthony's Messenger* 76:51-55, Nov. 1968.           A-38
Abortion and the law.  *Newsweek* 72:82-83, Dec. 2,
   1968.                                                                  A-39
Abortion and the law.  St. John-Stevas, Norman,
   *Dublin Review* 241:274-299, Winter 1967.            A-40
Abortion and the law.  *Tulane Law Review* 43:834-
   836, June 1969.                                                     A-41
Abortion and the Lords.  *New Statesman* 74:489,
   Oct. 20, 1967.                                                      A-42
Abortion and the sick mind.  *America* 113:37-38,
   July 10, 1965.                                                      A-43
Abortion and the soul.  O'Mahony, Patrick, *Month*
   38:45-50, July 1967.                                             A-44
Abortion as birth control.  *Medical Moral News-*

letter, 3:5, Jan. 1967. A-45

Abortion backlash. McKerron, Jane, New Statesman
78:5-6, July 4, 1969. A-46

Abortion: battle of emotions. Economist 222:914,
Mar. 11, 1967. A-47

Abortion can be costly. America 116:411-412, Mar.
25, 1967. A-48

Abortion: can doctors cope? McKerron, Jane, New
Statesman 75:166, Feb. 9, 1968. A-49

Abortion, Catholics and the law. St. John-Stevas,
Norman, Catholic World 206:149-152, Jan. 1968 A-50

Abortion clinic ethnography. Ball, Donald, Social
Problems 14:293-301, Winter 1967. A-51

Abortion compromise and ecumenism. Morriss,
Frank, Social Justice Review 60:264-265, Dec.
1967. A-52

Abortion, conscience and the law. O'Brien, R.,
Tablet 222:411-412, Apr. 27, 1968. A-53

Abortion debate and tough ecumenism. America
116:336, Mar. 11, 1967. A-54

Abortion debate. Bennett, John, Christianity in
Crisis 27:47-48, Mar. 20, 1967; 113-115, May
15. A-55

Abortion Decision. Granfield, David, Doubleday,
1969. A-56

Abortion for whom? New Republic 161:12, Oct. 25,
1969. A-57

Abortion, gas embolus and sudden death. Hibbard,
L., California Medicine 110:305-308, Apr. 1969. A-58

Abortion Handbook. Phelan, Lanna, Contact Press,
1969. A-59

Abortion in modern times. Munson, H., Renewal

13

7:9-10, Feb. 1967. A-60

Abortion in perspective. Gould, Donald, New Statesman 78:42-43, July 11, 1969. A-61

Abortion in the United States. Calderone, Mary,
Planned Parenthood Seminar, 1958. A-62

Abortion issue. America 115:406, Oct. 8, 1966. A-63

Abortion issues clouded. Hoyt, Robert, National
Catholic Reporter 3:1, Sept. 13, 1967. A-64

Abortion: Japan. Harrington, Paul, Linacre Quarterly 36:139-143, May 1969. A-65

Abortion: Law, Choice and Morality. Callahan, Daniel, Holt, 1970. A-66

Abortion law reform. Catholic Lawyer 14:180-184,
Summer 1968. A-67

Abortion law reform seen in New York. National
Catholic Reporter 5:3, Jan. 22, 1969. A-68

Abortion law: various approaches. American Journal
of Public Health 57:1906-1947, Nov. 1967. A-69

Abortion Laws. Wasmuth, Carl, Cleveland State
Law Review 18:503-509, Sept. 1969. A-70

Abortion laws and the courts. America 121:515, Nov.
29, 1969. A-71

Abortion: Legal and Illegal. Kummer, Jerome, auth-
or, Santa Monica, Cal., 1967. A-72

Abortion legislation and litigation. Catholic Lawyer
15:106-123, Spring 1969. A-73

Abortion legislation and the establishment clause.
Catholic Lawyer 15:108-111, Spring 1969. A-74

Abortion: mediate vs immediate animation. Donceel,
Joseph, Continuum 5:(5) 167-171, Spring 1967. A-75

Abortion, medicine and due process. Louisell,
David, UCLA Law Review 16:233-240, Feb. 1969. A-76

14

Abortion on Trial. Shaw, Russell, Pflaum, 1969.     A-77

Abortion--or compulsory pregnancy. Hardin, Garrett,
  Journal of Marriage and the Family 30:246-251,
  May 1968.                                         A-78

Abortion picture in Britain. America 116:490-491,
  Apr. 1, 1967.                                     A-79

Abortion problem and statistics. America 114:
  Apr. 16, 1966.                                    A-80

Abortion question. Byrn, Robert, Catholic Lawyer
  11:316-322, Fall 1965.                            A-81

Abortion reform. Shaw, Russell, Columbia 48:20-22,
  Nov. 1968.                                        A-82

Abortion reform in Michigan. Wayne Law Review 14:
  1006-1007, Summer 1968.                           A-83

Abortion statement by Illinois bishops. Catholic
  Mind 67:59-64, Mar. 1969.                         A-84

Abortion statement by New Jersey bishops. Catholic
  Mind 66:4-5, June 1968.                           A-85

Abortion, the law and defective children. Suffolk
  University Law Review 3:225-230, Spring 1969.     A-86

Abortion, the law and the common good. Hellegers,
  Andre, Catholic Mind 65:28-39, Dec. 1967.        A-87

Abortion: two sides. Mayhewn, Leonard Ecumenist
  5:75-77, July 1967.                               A-88

Abortion used as birth control. Carr, Aidan, Homiletic and Pastoral Review 67:523-525, Mar. 1967.  A-89

Abortion, who should decide? Kramer, Herbert,
  Liguorian 56:33-36, Jan. 1968.                    A-90

Abortionist rhetoric. America 120:639, May 31,
  1969.                                             A-91

Abortion's crucial question. Lyons, Bernard, Extension 62:17-21, Oct. 1967.                      A-92

15

Abortions for all? Newsweek 73:104, Mar. 17, 1969. A-93

Abortions: ten years experience. Wall, L. A.,
American Journal of Obstetrics and Gynecology 79:
510-515, 1960. A-94

Absolutes in Moral Theology? Curran, Charles E.,
Corpus, 1968. A-95

Action on the Streets. Carney, Frank, Association
Press, 1969. A-96

Adam, Corinna. Disappointed prophetess, New
Statesman 78:177-178, Aug. 8, 1969. A-97

Adler, Nathan. The antinomian personality, Psychiatry 31:(4) 325-338, 1968. A-98

Adolescence. Sebald, Hans, Appleton-Century-Croft,
1968. A-99

Adolescence. Usdin, Gene, Lippincott, 1969. A-100

Adolescence: Contemporary Studies. Winder, Alvin,
American Book Co., 1968. A-101

Afterthoughts. Hoyt, Robert, National Catholic
Reporter 3:10, Sept. 20, 1967. A-102

AID's family planning strategy. Ravenholt, R.
Science 163:124, Jan. 10, 1969. A-103

Alberta sterilization act. Weijer, John, University
of Toronto Law Journal 19:424-429, 1969. A-104

Alexander, Theron. Children and Adolescents,
Atherton, 1969. A-105

All they talk about is sex, sex, sex. Buckley,
Tom, New York Times Magazine 28-29, April
20, 1969. A-106

Almost an aggiornamento. America 117:27-28, July
8, 1967. A-107

Alverson, Charles. A Minority's plea, Wall Street
Journal 172:1, July 17, 1968. A-108

16

Amendment of the abortion law.   Noonan, John,
    Catholic Lawyer 15:124-135, Spring 1969.    A-108a

American Civil Liberties Union.   Policy Guide, 1967.  A-109

American Institute of Family Living, 5287 Sunset
    Blvd. Los Angeles, Calif. , 90027.   Family Life
    (newsletter).    A-110

AMA policy on therapeutic abortion.   American Med-
    ical Assn. Journal 201:544, Aug. 14, 1967.    A-111

No entry    A-112

Analysis of proposed changes in Ohio.   University
    of Cincinnati Law Review 37:340-345, Spring 1968.  A-113

And baby makes one.   Francoeur, Robert, Critic 28:
    34-41, Nov. 1969.    A-114

Anderson, E. Psychiatric indications for termination
    of pregnancy, Journal of Psychosomatic Research
    10:127-134, 1966.    A-115

Andrews, James. Jesuit denies abortion in early
    stages is immoral, National Catholic Reporter
    5:6, Nov. 27, 1968.    A-116

Andrews, James.   Twilight-zone dialogue, Ave
    Maria 105:4-5, Apr. 29, 1967.    A-117

Angrist, Shirley.   Study of sex roles, Journal of
    Social Issues 25:215-232, Jan. 1969.    A-118

Annual battle over abortion laws.   Shaw, Russell,
    National Catholic Reporter 5:1, Mar. 19, 1969.  A-118a

Antenatal euthanasia.   DeWeber, L. , New England
    Journal of Medicine 280:1248, May 29, 1969.    A-119

Antinomian personality, Adler, Nathan, Psychiatry
    31 (4) 325-338, 1968.    A-120

Antithesis of the practice of medicine.   Lauth, Ed-
    ward, Catholic Mind 66:20-27, Mar. 1968.    A-121

No entry    A-122

Apologia pro Vita Humana. Hay, Gerald, <u>Homiletic</u>
   <u>and Pastoral Review</u> 70:283-286, Jan. 1970.          A-123
<u>Appalachian Fertility Decline</u>. DeJong, Gordon,
   University of Kentucky Press, 1968.                       A-124
Are babies consumer durables? Blake, Judith, <u>Pop-</u>
   <u>ulation Studies</u> 22:5-25, Mar. 1968.                A-125
Are religious magazines obscene? Shea, Terence,
   <u>Seminar</u> 14:23-27, Dec. 1969.                       A-126
Armijo, Rolando. Aspects of abortion in Chile,
   <u>Public Health Reports</u> 83:41-48, Jan. 1968.        A-127
Artificial fertilization and pregnancy. Sillo-Seidl,
   Georg, <u>Medical Gynaecology and Sociology</u> 4:
   238-240, Sept. 1969.                                      A-128
Ashley-Montagu, M. A. <u>Life Before Birth</u>, New
   American Library, 1965.                                   A-129
Ashley-Montagu, M. A. <u>Sex, Man and Society</u>,
   Putnam, 1969.                                             A-130
Aspects of abortion in Chile. Armijo, Rolando,
   <u>Public Health Reports</u> 83:41-48, Jan. 1968.        A-131
Aspects of the moral question. McCormick, Richard,
   <u>America</u> 117:716-719, Dec. 9, 1967.                A-132
Association for the Study of Abortion, 120 W. 57th
   St., New York, N. Y. 10019. <u>Newsletter</u>.           A-133
Authority, usury and contraception. <u>Insight</u> 6:
   29-42, Fall, 1967.                                        A-134
Ayd, Frank. Liberal abortion laws, <u>America</u> 120:
   130-132, Feb. 1, 1969.                                    A-135
Ayd, Frank. Liberal abortion laws, <u>American Eccles-</u>
   <u>iastical Review</u> 158:73-91, Feb. 1968.             A-136
Ayd, Frank. Liberal abortion laws, <u>Marriage</u> 51:
   40-43, June 1969.                                         A-137.
Ayd, Frank. Medical moral problems in a troubled

society, <u>NCEA Bulletin</u> 66:97-102, Aug. 1969.        A-138

Ayd, Frank.   The pill--does it cause abortion?   <u>Na-</u>
   <u>tional Catholic Reporter</u>, Aug 4, 1965, page 6.      A-139

Babi Yar and babies. Curran, Richard, <u>Linacre</u>
<u>Quarterly</u> 35:240-242, Nov. 1968.                    B-1

Bachelor, Evelyn. <u>Teen Conflicts,</u> Diablo Press,
1968.                                                    B-2

Backer, Matt. The decision to kill, <u>Social Justice</u>
<u>Review</u> 60:119-121, July 1967.                     B-3

Baird, Dugald. <u>Living with the Pill,</u> London, Times
Newspapers, 1969.                                        B-4

Bakalar, Lorraine. Re: sex education, <u>Visitor,</u>
Jan. 25, 1970, Page 11.                                  B-5

Baker, N. Septic abortion and maternal mortality,
<u>Journal of the American Osteopath Association</u>
68:807-814, 1969.                                        B-6

Ball, Donald. Abortion clinic ethnography, <u>Social</u>
<u>Problems</u> 14:293-301, Winter 1967.                 B-7

Barclay, Lillian. Group approach to young unwed
mothers, <u>Social Casework</u> 50:379-384, July 1969.  B-8

Barr, O. <u>Christian New Morality</u>, Oxford University
Press, 1969.                                             B-9

Barr, Stringfellow. Second edition: consulting the
Romans, <u>Center Magazine</u> 3:39-51, Jan. 1970.      B-10

Barth, Alan. Time to license parents, <u>Los Angeles</u>
<u>Times,</u> Dec. 28, 1969. opinion.                    B-11

Baseline for criminal abortions? <u>Lancet</u> 2:309,
Aug. 9, 1969.                                            B-12

Bates, Jerome. <u>Criminal Abortion</u>, Thomas, 1964.  B-13

Battle against ignorance, superstition and moralizing.

Harris, Alan, New Statesman 77:284-287, Feb. 28, 1969.                                                                B-14

Baum, Gregory. Catholic response (to Darst-Forgue), Ecumenist 7:90-92, Sept. 1969.                                   B-15

Baum, Gregory. Right to dissent, Commonweal 88:553-554, Aug. 23, 1968.                                               B-16

Be Not Content. Craddock, William, Doubleday, 1970.                                                                  B-17

Bedroom should not be within the province of the law. Goodman, Irv, California Western Law Review 4:115-131, Spring 1968.        B-18

Beginning of life as an ethical problem. Buss, Martin, Journal of Religion 47:244-255, July 1967.                    B-19

Bennett, John. Abortion debate, Christianity in Crisis 27:47-48, Mar. 20, 1967; 113-115, May 15.                     B-20

Benson, Leonard. Fatherhood, Random, 1968.          B-21

Bentley, Eric. Naked American, New Republic 161: 31-34, Aug. 16, 1969.                                               B-22

Berelson, Bernard. Family Planning Programs, Basic Books, 1969.                                                      B-23

Berg, Roland. Trans-sexuals: male or female? Look 34:29-31, Jan. 27, 1970.                                           B-24

Bernard, Jessie. Sex Game, Prentice-Hall, 1968.     B-25

Berrill, Norman. The Person in the Womb, Dodd, 1968.                                                                 B-26

Berry, Leonard. Il Papa and the pill, Commonweal 90:44-46, Mar. 28, 1969.                                            B-27

Best Law: no law? America 117:292, Sept. 23, 1967.                                                                   B-28

Betrayal of the poor. Harrington, Michael, Atlantic

225:71-74, Jan. 1970. B-29

Beyond Birth Control. Callahan, Sidney, Sheed and
Ward, 1968. B-30

Bibliography of fertility control. Tietze, Christopher, National Committee on Maternal Health
#23, 1965. B-31

Bier, William. Marriage: Psychological and Moral
Approach, Fordham University Press, 1969. B-32

Bill C-150. Parker, Graham, Criminal Law Quarterly 11:267-269, May 1969. B-33

Bill, H. E. Manual of clinical contraception, North
Carolina Medical Journal 30:169-182, May 1969. B-34

Billingsley, Andrew. Black Families in White America, Prentice-Hall, 1968. B-35

Biological Time Bomb. Taylor, Gordon, World,
1969. B-36

Biology and Man. Simpson, George, Harcourt, 1969. B-37

Biology and the Christian faith. Smith, B., Christianity Today 13:11-14, Apr. 11, 1969; 11-14,
Apr. 25, 1969. B-38

Biology of the reproductive act, Hayes, Thomas,
Insight 6:12-19, Fall 1967. B-39

Birch Society's attack on sex education answered.
Michigan Medicine 68:518-522, May 1969. B-40

Birth Control and Love. Guttmacher, Alan, Macmillan, 1969. B-41

Birth control and population. Ghorbani, F. S.,
Medical Gynecology and Sociology 4:228-233,
Sept. 1969. B-42

Birth control commission: conflict. Riga, Peter,
Pastoral Life 16:281-290, May 1968. B-43

Birth Control Debate. Hoyt, Robert, National

22

Catholic Reporter, 1968.                                    B-44

Birth control in Chile.  Gonzalez, Gerado, Catholic
    Mind 113:29-34, Dec. 1969.                             B-45

Birth control in Jewish Law.  Feldman, David
    N. Y. University Press, 1969.                          B-46

Birth control knowledge and attitudes among unmar-
    ried pregnant adolescents.  Furstenberg, Frank,
    Journal of Marriage and the Family 31:34-42,
    Feb. 1969.                                             B-47

Birth control now, country by country.  U. S. News
    and World Report 66:49-52, Mar. 17, 1969.             B-48

Birth Controllers.  Fryer, Peter, Secker and War-
    burg, 1965.                                            B-49

Birth regulation and situation ethics.  Gerharz,
    George, Listening 3:208-213, Autumn 1968.             B-50

Bishops of Canada propose alternative.  National
    Catholic Reporter 4:5, Feb. 14, 1968.                 B-51

The Bishops of Illinois.  Statement on abortion,
    Catholic Mind 67:59-64, May 1969.                     B-52

Bishops ought to marry.  Fichter, Joseph, Common-
    weal 88:289-291, May 24, 1968.                        B-53

Bishops--U. S.  Collective pastoral on "Humanae
    Vitae," The Pope Speaks 13:377-405, #4, 1969.         B-54

Bjork, Robert.  International perspective in sex ed-
    ucation, Journal of School Health 39:525-537,
    Oct. 1969.                                             B-55

Black Families in White America.  Billingsley,
    Andrew, Prentice-Hall, 1968.                          B-56

Blake, Judith.  Are babies consumer durables?
    Population Studies 22:5-25, Mar. 1968.                B-57

Blatt, Burton.  Politics of human welfare, Journal
    of Education 152:45-50, Oct. 1969.                    B-58

                        23

Blueprints, D. N. A. and abortion. Hardin, Garrett, Medical Opinion and Review, 1967. B-59

Bourgeois-Pichat, Jean. Population Growth and Development. International Conciliation 556:1-81, Jan. 1966. B-60

Boys and Sex. Pomeroy, Wardell, Delacorte Press, 1968. B-61

Bradway, John. Progress in Family Law, Annals of the American Academy of Political and Social Science 383, May 1969. B-62

Brazelton, T. Infants and Mothers, Delacorte, 1969. B-63

Breig, Joseph. Religious liberty and abortion, Ave Maria 103:20, Apr. 23, 1966. B-64

Broderick, Carlfred. Sex, Society and the Individual, Johns Hopkins Press, 1969. B-65

Brown, J. Abortion and guffaws for chastity, New England Journal of Medicine 281:276, July 31, 1969. B-66

Brungs, Robert. Danger of abortion, St. Louis Review, Jan. 16, 1970, p. 11. B-67

Buckley, Tom. All they talk about is sex, sex, sex, New York Times Magazine 28-29, Apr. 20, 1969. B-68

Buckley, William. Sophists will play, National Review 21:1182, Nov. 18, 1969. B-69

Bukowski, Charles. Notes of a Dirty Old Man, Essex House (N. Hollywood) 1969. B-70

Burton, Arthur. Encounter, Jossey-Bass, 1969. B-71

Buss, Martin. Beginning of life as an ethical problem, Journal of Religion 47:244-255, July 1967. B-72

Byrn, Robert. Abortion: a legal view, <u>Commonweal</u>
85:679-680, Mar. 17, 1967.                              B-73

Byrn, Robert. The abortion question, <u>Catholic</u>
<u>Lawyer</u> 11:316-322, Fall 1965.                    B-74

Byrn, Robert. Demythologizing abortion reform,
<u>Catholic Lawyer</u> 14:180-189, Summer 1968.         B-75

Byrn, Robert. The new theology of abortion reformers, <u>Family Digest</u> 22:6-11, Feb. 1967.      B-76

Byrne, Richard. What are the rights of the unborn child? <u>Marriage</u> 49:16-21, Feb. 1967.      B-77

Calderone, Mary. <u>Abortion in the United States,</u>
Planned Parenthood Seminar, 1958.                     C-1

Calderone, Mary. Interview, <u>Look,</u> Mar. 8, 1966.     C-2

Calderone, Mary. Sex questions that bother boys,
<u>Seventeen</u> 27:80-81, July 1968.                    C-3

Calderone, Mary. <u>Introduction; Conception, Birth
and Contraception,</u> McGraw-Hill, 1969.               C-4

Calderone, Mary. Sex, religion and mental health,
<u>Journal of Religion and Health</u> 6:195-203, July
1967.                                                    C-5

Calderone, Mary. <u>Sexual Health and Family Planning,</u> American Public Health Association, 1968.     C-6

Calderone, Mary. Sexuality and the college student,
<u>Journal of the American College Health Associa-
tion</u> 17:189-193, Feb. 1969.                         C-7

Calderone, Mary. Special report: SIECUS in 1969,
<u>Journal of Marriage and the Family</u> 31:674-676,
Nov. 1969.                                               C-8

California abortion law unconstitutional. <u>San Diego
Evening Tribune,</u> Jan. 10, 1970, p. 1 (UPI dispatch)                                                   C-9

California therapeutic abortion act. <u>Hastings Law
Journal</u> 19:242-250, Nov. 1967.                      C-10

California's new therapeutic abortion act. Charles,
Alan, <u>UCLA Law Review</u> 15:1-31, Dec. 1967.       C-11

California's new therapeutic abortion act. Leavy,
Zad, <u>UCLA Law Review</u> 15:1-31, Nov. 1967.        C-12

Callahan, Daniel. Abortion: Law, Choice and Morality, Holt, 1970.     C-13

Callahan, Daniel. The Catholic Case for Contraception, Macmillan, 1969.     C-14

Callahan, Daniel. Uncertain future of sex, National Catholic Reporter 5:8, Feb. 12, 1969.     C-15

Callahan, Sidney. Beyond Birth Control, Sheed and Ward, 1968.     C-16

Callahan, Sidney. Human sexuality in a time of change, Christian Century 85:1077-1080, Aug. 28, 1968, 1310, Oct. 16, 1968.     C-17

Cameron, W. Survival against odds, Journal of the Kansas Medical Society 70:326-327, July 1969.     C-18

Canada debates abortion, homosexuality. Fleck, J. C., Christian Century 86:354-358, Mar. 12, 1969.     C-19

Canavan, Francis. Church's right to speak out, Catholic Mind 65:13-16, Apr. 1967.     C-20

Carlova, John. Legal abortions, an unholy mess in Britain, Medical Economics, 270-289, Oct. 13, 1969.     C-21

Carney, Frank. Action on the Streets, Association Press, 1969.     C-22

Caron, Wilfrid. New York abortion reform, Catholic Lawyer 14:180-213, Summer 1968.     C-23

Carr, Aidan. Abortion used as birth control, Homiletic and Pastoral Review 67:523-525, Mar. 1967.     C-24

Carr, Aidan. The Church's doctrinal decisions on abortion, Homiletic and Pastoral Review 67:610-611, Apr. 1967.     C-25

Carr, Aidan. The pill: abortion or contraception? Homiletic and Pastoral Review 66:340-341, Jan. 1966.     C-26

Carr, Aidan. Pressure to change abortion laws, Homiletic and Pastoral Review 67:702-704, May 1967.                                                    C-27

Carter, L. Population crisis, Science 166:722-726, Nov. 7, 1969.                                        C-28

Case for Legalized Abortion Now. Guttmacher, Alan, Diablo Press, 1967.                          C-29

Catechism of modern man. St Paul Editions, 1967, pp. 350, 388.                                  C-30

Catholic Case for Contraception. Callahan, Daniel, Macmillan, 1969.                              C-31

Catholic Church and abortion. Noonan, John, Dublin Review 241:300-345, Winter 1967.    C-32

Catholic doctors and abortion bills. Social Justice Review 60:243, Nov. 1967.                    C-33

Catholic moral teaching and abortion laws in America. Drinan, Robert, Proceedings, American Catholic Philosophical Association 23:118-130, 1968.                                             C-34

Catholic position on abortion. Daily, Thomas, Linacre Quarterly 34:218-220, Aug. 1967.    C-35

Catholics U.S.A. Liu, William, Wiley, 1970.       C-36

Cavanagh, John. Psychiatric indications for the use of contraceptives, Linacre Quarterly 36:92-99, May 1969.                                             C-37

Celibacy: the Necessary Option. Frein, George, Herder and Herder, 1968.                          C-38

Champlin, Joseph. Sex and confession, Pastoral Life 16:, articles in May, June and July issues. 1969.                                                 C-39

Chandler, Russell. New Look at abortion, Christianity Today 11:28-30, Sept. 29, 1967.        C-40

28

Changing American attitudes toward prostitution.
Riegel, Robert, Journal of the History of Ideas
29:437-452, July 1968.                                    C-41

The changing family.   World Justice 9:149-227, Dec.
1967.                                                     C-42

Changing reference groups and premarital sex.
Teeven, James, Dissertation Abstracts 29:9A-
3242, 1969.                                               C-43

Chapman, Arthur.   Sexual Maneuvers and Stratagems,
Putnam, 1969.                                             C-44

Chappell, D.   Public attitudes, Australian Law
Journal 42:120-175, Aug. 1968.                            C-45

Charles, Alan. California's new therapeutic abortion act, UCLA Law Review 15:1-31, Dec.
1967.                                                     C-46

Chaskel, R. Illegitimacy: dimensions of prevention,
Social Casework 50:95-101, Feb. 1969.                     C-47

Chesser, Eustace.   Love and the Married Woman,
Putnam, 1969.                                             C-48

Child, his birth without permission.   Hall, Robert,
Saturday Review 52:59-60, Mar. 1, 1969.                   C-49

Children and Adolescents.   Alexander, Theron,
Atherton, 1969.                                           C-50

Children--choice or chance?  Wrage, Karl, Fortress Press, 1969.                                         C-51

Children's Bureau HEW.   Some facts and figures
about adolescents, U.S. Gov't Pub. 1968 FS
17.202:ad 7.                                              C-52

Children's rights.  Drinan, Robert, America 122:
4-5, Jan. 10, 1970.                                       C-53

Chilman, Catherine.  Fertility and poverty, Journal
of Marriage and the Family 30:207-227, May 1968. C-54

Chow, Lien-Pin. Correlates of IUD termination in
a mass family planning program, Millbank Memorial Fund Quarterly 46:215-235, Apr. 1968.     C-55

Christian approach to the ethics of abortion. Gustafson, James, Dublin Review 241:346-364, Winter 1967.     C-56

Christian love and the loss of intimacy. White,
W. D., University of Portland Review 21 #2,
13-22, Fall 1969.     C-57

Christian morals. McCormick, Richard, America
122:5-6, Jan 10, 1970.     C-58

Christian New Morality. Barr, O., Oxford University press, 1969.     C-59

Christian re-examination of sex. McLaughlin,
John, St. Anthony's Messenger, articles Apr. -
Aug. 1968, Jan. and Apr. 1969.     C-60

Church and the urban crisis. Dearden, John,
Pastoral Life 16:375-380, June 1968.     C-61

Church Assembly Board for Social Responsibility.
Abortion: an Ethical Discussion, Church Information Office, Westminster 1965.     C-62

The Church in the Modern World #27. The Sixteen Documents of Vatican II, St. Paul Editions,
1967, p. 539.     C-63

Church of promise. Wright, John, Columbia 50:
17-26, Jan. 1970.     C-64

Church's attitude toward sex distorted by Augustine. Thomas, F., U. S. Catholic 32:58, Oct.
1966.     C-65

Church's doctrinal decisions on abortion. Carr,
Aidan, Homiletic and Pastoral Review 67:610-
611, Apr. 1967.     C-66

Church's right to speak out.   Canavan, Francis,
   Catholic Mind 65:13-16,  Apr. 1967.        C-67

Cittadini, E.  Experience with sequential estrogen-
   progestin treatments, International Journal of
   Fertility 14:180-187,  Apr. 1969.        C-68

Civil liberties and homosexuality.   Social Action
   34:5-47,  Dec. 1967.        C-69

Clanton, G.  Understanding sex in the age of the pill,
   Christian Century 86:187,  Feb. 5,  1969.        C-70

Clayton, Richard.   Religious orthodoxy and premarital sex, Social Forces 47:469-474,  June 1969.        C-71

Clergy and abortions.   Time 94:82,  Nov. 28,  1969.        C-72

Clinical safety of oral contraceptives.   Schrogie,
   John, FDA Papers 3:5,  June 1969.        C-73

Cohen, Carl.   Sex, birth control and human life,
   Ethics 79:251-262,  July 1969.        C-74

College marriages.   Zarrella, Mary, Marriage
   51:60-65,  May 1969.        C-75

Colorado first.   National Catholic Reporter 3:5,
   Apr. 19, 1967.        C-76

Colorado story.   Heller, A. , American Journal
   of Psychiatry 125:809-816,  1968.        C-77

Colorado's new abortion law.   University of Colorado
   Law Review 40:297-303,  Winter 1968.        C-78

Coming to terms.   Time 94:82,  Oct. 24,  1969.        C-79

Commentary on psychiatric indications for the use
   of contraceptives.   Paganelli, Vitale, Linacre
   Quarterly 36:197-201,  Aug. 1969.        C-80

Common Sense Sex.   Mazur, Ronald, Beacon
   Press, 1968.        C-81

Commonweal.   Abortion, a symposium, Commonweal, June 30, 1967.        C-82

Communal living. Shaffer, Helen, Editorial Research Reports 2:5 Aug. 6, 1969. C-83

Communications in Family Planning. Dandekar, Kumudini, Asia Publishing House, 1967. C-84

Conception, Birth and Contraception. Demarest, Robert, McGraw-Hill, 1969. C-85

Concern for the Soviet family. Gorkin, A., Soviet Review 10:47-53, Fall 1969. C-86

Conference without consensus. McCormick, Richard, America 117:716-719, Sept. 23, 1967. C-87

Conflict of Generations. Feuer, Lewis, Basic Books, 1969. C-88

Contemporary attitudes of the Roman Catholic Church toward abortion. Wassmer, Thomas, Journal of Religion and Health 7:311-323, Oct. 1968. C-89

Contemporary Problems in Moral Theology. Curran, Charles E., Fides, 1970. C-90

Contemporary Protestant thinking. Drinan, Robert, America 117:713-715, Dec. 9, 1967. C-91

Contraception. Noonan, John, Harvard University Press, 1965. C-92

Contraception and abortion. Christianity Today 13:3-12, Nov. 8, 1968. C-93

Contraception, Authority and Dissent. Curran, Charles E., Herder and Herder, 1969. C-94

Contraceptive Practice. Peel, John, Cambridge University Press, 1969. C-95

Contraceptives and the single person. Walters, Orville, Christianity Today 13:16-17, Dec. 8, 1968. C-96

Control of fertility. Hoagland, H., Science 161:

32

1261. Sept. 20, 1968.       C-97

Conversations on the new eroticism. Time 94:64-
65, July 11, 1969.       C-98

Conway, John. The natural law argument, Marriage 49:44-49, May, 1967.       C-99

Cooke, R. The Terrible Choice, Bantam, 1969.       C-100

Correlates of IUD termination in a mass family
planning program. Chow, Lien-Pin, Millbank
Memorial Fund Quarterly 46:215-235, Apr. 1968.       C-101

Court recognizes rights. St. Anthony's Messenger
75:11, Jan. 1968.       C-102

Craddock, William. Be Not Content, Doubleday
1970.       C-103

Creation of the human soul. Reaney, William,
Benziger Brothers 1932.       C-104

Crews, Frederick. Love in the western world,
Partisan Review 33:272-287, Spring 1967.       C-105

Criminal Abortion. Bates, Jerome, Thomas, 1964.       C-106

Criminal Abortion. Zawadzki, Edward, Thomas,
1964.       C-107

Criminal law, need for reform. Kentucky Law
Journal 57:591-595, 1968-1969.       C-108

Crime of abortion in Canon Law. Huser, Roger,
Catholic University Press, 1942.       C-109

Crisis of morality. Kogler, James, Focus on
Hope, 1970.       C-110

Cross, Wilford. Morality today, Churchman 184:
6-7, Jan. 1970.       C-111

Cross-cultural family research. Journal of Marriage and the Family 31:203-207, May 1969.       C-112

Crossman and the pill. Gould, Donald, New Statesman 77:686-687. May 16, 1969.       C-113

Culture and Commitment. Mead, Margaret, Double-
day, 1969.                                                    C-114

Curran, Charles E. Absolutes in Moral Theology?
Corpus, 1968.                                                 C-115

Curran, Charles E. Contemporary Problems in
Moral Theology, Fides, 1970.                                  C-116

Curran, Charles E. Contraception, Authority and
Dissent, Herder and Herder, 1969.                            C-117

Curran, Charles E. Dissent In and For the Church,
Sheed and Ward, 1970.                                        C-118

Curran, Charles E. Masturbation: an objectively
grave matter, Proceedings, Catholic Theological
Society of America 21:95-109, 1966.                          C-119

Curran, Charles E. Sexuality and sin, Homiletic
and Pastoral Review 68:1005-1014, Sept. 1968;
27-34, Oct. 1968.                                            C-120

Curran, Richard. Babi Yar and babies, Linacre
Quarterly 35:240-242, Nov. 1968.                             C-121

Curran, Richard. The quiet murder, Linacre
Quarterly 344-348, Nov. 1966.                                C-122

Curran, W. Public health and the law, American
Journal of Public Health 59:1434-1435, Aug.
1969.                                                        C-123

Current abortion laws. George, B., Western Re-
serve Press, 1967.                                           C-124

Current theology. McCormick, Richard, Theological
Studies 30:635-692, Dec. 1969.                               C-125

Cushner, Irvin. Induced abortion in contemporary
medical practice, Journal of Religion and Health
7:324-332, Oct. 1968.                                        C-126

34

Dailey, Thomas.   Catholic position on abortion,
  Linacre Quarterly 34:218-222, Aug. 1967.                D-1
Daly, Cahal.  Morals, Law and Life, Scepter,
  1966.                                                   D-2
Damned millions.  Pospishil, Victor, Homiletic
  and Pastoral Review 69:95-104, Nov. 1968.               D-3
Dandekar, Kumudini.  Communication in Family
  Planning, Asia Publishing House, 1967.                  D-4
Danger of abortion.  Brungs, Robert, St. Louis
  Review Jan. 16, 1970, p. 11.                            D-5
D'Antonio, William.  Pills, coils and abortion,
  Commonweal 86:193-194, May 5, 1967.                     D-6
Darst, David.  Sexuality on the island earth,
  Ecumenist 7:81-87, Sept. 1969.                          D-7
Dartmouth Convocation.  Great issues of con-
  science in modern medicine, Hanover, Sept.
  8-10, 1960.                                             D-8
Davis, K. Population policy: will current programs
  succeed?  Science 158:730-739, 1967.                    D-9
Day, Lincoln.  Family size in industrialized coun-
  tries, Journal of Marriage and the Family 31:
  242-251 May 1969.                                       D-10
Dearden, John.  The Church and the urban crisis,
  Pastoral Life 16:375-380, June 1968.                    D-11
Dear Doctor Hip Pocrates.  Schoenfeld, Eugene,
  Grove, 1969.                                            D-12

35

Debate on legalized abortion.  Kennedy, Jeremiah,
　　Sign 46:34-35,  June 1967.　　　　　　　　　　　　　D-13

Decent and Indecent.  Spock, Benjamin, McCalls,
　　1970.　　　　　　　　　　　　　　　　　　　　　　D-14

Decision to kill.  Backet, Matt, Social Justice Re-
　　view 60:119-121,  July, 1967.　　　　　　　　　　　D-15

Deisher, R.  Young male prostitute, Pediatrics 43:
　　936-941, June, 1969.　　　　　　　　　　　　　　　D-16

DeJong, Gordon.  Appalachian Fertility Decline,
　　University of Kentucky Press, 1968.　　　　　　　　D-17

Delaunay, Albert, ed.  Man of Tomorrow, Double-
　　day, 1966.　　　　　　　　　　　　　　　　　　　D-18

Delaware's abortion reform.  Moyer, C., Delaware
　　Medical Journal 41:199, June, 1969.　　　　　　　　D-19

Demarest, Robert.  Conception, Birth and Contra-
　　ception, McGraw-Hill, 1969.　　　　　　　　　　　D-20

Demographic Yearbook.  United Nations Publications,
　　1969.　　　　　　　　　　　　　　　　　　　　　　D-21

Demythologizing abortion reform.  Byrn, Robert,
　　Catholic Lawyer 14:180, 189, Summer 1968.　　　　D-22

Deutsche, Ronald.  Key to Feminine Response in
　　Marriage, Random, 1968.　　　　　　　　　　　　　D-23

Developing Nations.  Isenberg, Irwin, H. W. Wil-
　　son., 1969.　　　　　　　　　　　　　　　　　　　D-24

Devine, George.  To Be a Man.  Prentice-Hall,
　　1969.　　　　　　　　　　　　　　　　　　　　　　D-25

De Weber, L.  Antenatal euthanasia, New England
　　Journal of Medicine 280-1248, May 29, 1969.　　　D-26

Diamond, Eugene.  The physician and the rights
　　of the unborn, Linacre Quarterly 34:174-181,
　　May, 1967.　　　　　　　　　　　　　　　　　　　D-27

Diamond, Eugene.  Who speaks for the fetus?

Linacre Quarterly 36:58062, Feb. 1969.          D-28

Diamond, James.   Humanizing the abortion debate,
    America, 121:36-39, July 19, 1969.          D-29

Diamond, Milton.   Perspectives in reproduction and
    sexual behavior.   Indiana Univ. Press, 1968.     D-30

Dictionary of Modern Sociology.   Hoult, Thomas,
    Little, Adams, 1969.                         D-31

Difficult delivery of new abortion laws.   New Eng-
    land Journal of Medicine 280:1240-1241, May
    29, 1969.                                    D-32

Difficult quest.   Giannella, Donald, Villanova Law
    Review 13:257-269, Winter 1968.              D-33

Disappointed prophetess.   Adam, Corina, New
    Statesman 78:177-178, Aug. 8, 1969.          D-34

Dissent in and for the Church.   Curran, Charles
    E., Sheed and Ward, 1970.                    D-35

Divorce and Remarriage.   Pospishil, Victor, Herder
    and Herder, 1967.                            D-36

Djerassi, Carl.   Prognosis for the development of
    new chemical birth control agents, Science 166:
    468-473, Oct. 24, 1969.                      D-37

Dr. Bowdler's Legacy.   Perrin, Noel, Atheneum,
    1969.                                        D-38

Doctor talks about abortion.   Rattner, Herbert,
    Catholic Mind 64:45050, May 1966.            D-39

Dollen, Charles.   In the service of life, Perspec-
    tives, May-June 1965.                        D-40

Dollen, Charles.   Rebuttal: three position papers
    on birth control, Priest 23:444-447, June 1967.   D-41

Dollen, Charles.   Storm Center: SIECUS, Pas-
    toral Life 19:18-21, Feb. 1970.              D-42

Dollen, Charles.   Toward a Responsible Priesthood,

San Diego, Cal., Mercy Hospital (pamphlet)
1965.                                                              D-43

Donceel, Joseph.  Abortion: mediate vs immediate
animation, Continuum 5:167-171, Spring 1967.        D-44

Donceel, Joseph.  Philosophical Anthropology,
Sheed & Ward, 1967.                                        D-45

Dort, Nicholas.  Teen-age Masturbation, Los
Angeles, Spartan House, 1968.                            D-46

Drama of life before birth.  Life 58:65-77a, April
30, 1965.                                                           D-47

Draper, William.  Population still exploding, Global
Dialogue, 1:136-139, Oct. 1968.                          D-48

Drinan, Robert.  Catholic moral teaching and abortion laws in America, Proceedings, American
Catholic Philosophical Association 23:118-130,
1968.                                                                D-49

Drinan, Robert.  Children's rights, America 122:
4-5, Jan. 10, 1970.                                            D-50

Drinan, Robert.  Contemporary Protestant thinking,
America 117:713-715, Dec. 9, 1967.                    D-51

Drinan, Robert.  Morality of abortion laws, Catholic
Lawyer 14:190-198, Summer 1968.                      D-52

Drinan, Robert.  Right of the foetus to be born,
Dublin Review 241:365-381, Winter 1967.            D-53

Drinan, Robert.  Strategy on abortion.  America
116:177-179, Feb. 4, 1967.                                D-54

The drug revolution.  Playboy 17:53-74, Feb. 1970.   D-55

Drug use and the law.  Fort, Joel, Current 113:
4-13, Dec. 1969.                                              D-56

Due process of abortion.  Kutnerm, Luis, Minnesota
Law Review 53:1-10, Nov. 1968.                        D-57

Dunstan, Keith.  Wowsers: an Account of Prudery.

Cassell, 1968.                                             D-58

Duvall, Evelyn.  <u>About Sex and Growing Up,</u> Asso-
    ciation, 1968.                                         D-59

Early development of homosexuality.  Kremer, M.,
   American Journal of Psychiatry 126:91-96, July
   1969.                                                E-1
Easier abortion laws.  Shaw, Russell, National
   Catholic Reporter 5:3, July 16, 1969.               E-2
Ecology of Reproduction in Mammals.  Sadleir,
   R., Methuen, 1969.                                   E-3
Economic model of family planning and fertility.
   Schultz, T. P., Journal of Political Economy
   77:153-180, Mar. 1969.                               E-4
Education in human sexuality.  McLaughlin, John.
   America 121:494:497, Nov. 22, 1969.                  E-5
Education in sex education, McLaughlin, John,
   Catholic School Journal 69:16-18, Oct. 1969.         E-6
Edwards, John.  The Family and Change.  Knopf,
   1969.                                                E-7
Effective Patterns of Services to Unmarried Parents.
   Gallagher, Ursula, Health, Education and Wel-
   fare Dept., 1968.                                    E-8
Effective Services for Unmarried Parents.  National
   Council on Illegitimacy, 1969.                       E-9
Effects of oral contraceptives.  Kalman, S., Annual
   Review of Pharmacology 9:363-378, 1969.              E-10
Ehrensing, Rudolph.  The I.U.D: How It Works,
   National Catholic Reporter reprint 1966.             E-11
Ehrlich, D. Pakistani sterilization campaign,
   Science News 93:306, Mar. 30, 1968.                  E-12
40

Ehrlich, Paul.   Population, food and environment,
    Texas Quarterly 11:43-54, Summer, 1968.      E-13

Eickhoff, Andrew.   Psychoanalytical study of St.
    Paul's theology of sex.   Pastoral Psychology
    18:35-52, Apr. 1967.      E-14

Eighty-six percent of M. D. 's favor abortion changes.
    National Catholic Reporter 3:7, May 10, 1967.      E-15

Eliminate causes of abortion.   Tablet 221:192, Feb.
    18, 1967.      E-16

Ellis, Albert.   Sexual promiscuity in America,
    Annals of the American Academy of Political and
    Social Science, 378:58-67, July 1968.      E-17

Empirical response.   Stafford, J. F., Catholic
    Charities Review 51:10-13, Nov. 1967.      E-18

Encounter.   Burton, Arthur, Jossey-Bass, 1969.      E-19

Encyclical Humanae Vitae.   Von Hildebrand, Dietrich,
    Franciscan Herald Press, 1969.      E-20

End of the foreplay flick?   Film Quarterly 22:1-2,
    Summer, 1969.      E-21

Engler, Barbara.   Sexuality and knowledge in Sig-
    mund Freud, Philosophy Today 13:214-224, Fall
    1969.      E-22

English experience.   St. John-Stevas, Norman,
    America 117-707-709.   Dec. 9, 1967.      E-23

Equality for homosexuals.   Christian Century 85:
    111-112 Jan. 24, 1968.      E-24

Erotic Fantasies.   Kronhausen, Phyllis and Eber-
    hard, Grove, 1970.      E-25

Ethical and moral considerations.   Tobin, William,
    Homiletic and Pastoral Review 67:1023-1031,
    Sept. 1967; 68:48:58, Oct.      E-26

Ethical problems of abortion.   McDonough, Michael,

Irish Theological Quarterly 35:268-297, July
1968.                                                          E-27

Everything You Always Wanted to Know About Sex.
Reuben, McKay 1969.                                            E-28

Evolution in the law.  Whelan, Charles, America
122: 11-12, Jan. 10, 1970.                                     E-29

Evoy, John.  The man and the woman.  Sheed and
Ward, 1969.                                                    E-30

Expectant father protected.  Standard Law Review
14:901, 1962.                                                  E-31

Experience with sequential estrogen-progestin
treatments.  Cittadini, E., International Journal
of Fertility 14:180-187, Apr. 1969.                            E-32

Fahr, S.   Therapeutic abortion--the law, Journal
   of the Iowa Medical Society 59:197-200, Mar.
   1969.                                              F-1

Family and Change.   Edwards, John, Knopf, 1969.      F-2

Family Life (newsletter).   American Institute of
   Family Living, 5287 Sunset Blvd., Los Angeles,
   Cal., 90027.                                       F-3

Family Planning.   O. E. O.   PrEx 10. 23:6130-3.     F-4

Family planning and differential fertility.   Heerin,
   Henk, Journal of Marriage and the Family 31:
   588-595, Aug. 1969.                                F-5

Family planning and the reduction of the pregnancy
   loss rate.   McCalister, Donald, Journal of Marriage and the Family 31:668-673, Nov. 1969.        F-6

Family Planning in an Exploding Population.   O'Brien,
   John, Hawthorn, 1969.                              F-7

Family Planning in cross-national perspective.   Rainwater, Lee, Journal of Social Issues 23:1-194,
   Oct. 1967.                                         F-8

Family Planning in Taiwan.   Freedman, Ronald,
   Princeton University Press, 1969.                  F-9

Family Planning Methods: Report.   United Nations
   pub.  E/AC. 52/L. 65, 1969.                        F-10

Family Planning: Nationwide Opportunities.   Health,
   Education and Welfare 1968,  FSI. 2F21/2/968.      F-11

Family planning: needs and methods, Guttmacher,
   Alan, American Journal of Nursing 69:1229-1234,

June 1969.                                          F-12

Family Planning Programs. Berelson, Bernard,
    Basic Books, 1969.                               F-13

Family Planning Programmes. Report. United
    Nations. Asian Population Studies Series, #13.   F-14

Family planning situation in India. Ganguli, H.,
    Indian Journal of Social Work 29:233-239, 1969.  F-15

Family size in industrialized countries. Day,
    Lincoln, Journal of Marriage and the Family
    31:242-251, May 1969.                           F-16

Farmer, Richard. World Population. Indiana
    University Press 1968.                           F-17

Fatherhood. Benson, Leonard, Random, 1968.          F-18

Fathi, Asghar. Jewish and gentile norms, Phylon
    29:5-12, Spring 1968.                           F-19

Federal constitutional limitations. North Carolina
    Law Review 46:730-737, June 1968.               F-20

Federal Court voids abortion law. Social Justice
    Review 62:273, Dec. 1969.                        F-21

FDA group labels the pill safe. American Druggist
    160:31-32, Sept. 22, 1969.                      F-22

Feldman, David. Birth control in Jewish law. N.Y.
    Univ. Press, 1969.                              F-23

Female homosexuality. Harvey, John, Linacre
    Quarterly 36:100-106, May 1969.                 F-24

Feminized Male. Sexton, Patricia, Random, 1969.     F-25

Ferm, Deane. Sweden, sex and the college student,
    Religious Education 64:53-60, Jan. 1969.        F-26

Ferris, Paul. Nameless: abortion in Britain Today.
    Hutchinson, 1966.                               F-27

Fertility after operations of extrauterine preg-
    nancies. Kucera, E., International Journal of

Fertility 14:127-129, Apr. 1969. F-28

Fertility and poverty. Chilman, Catherine, Journal
of Marriage and the Family 30: 207-227, May
1968. F-29

Feuer, Lewis. Conflict of Generations, Basic Books,
1969. F-30

Fichter, Joseph H. Bishops ought to marry, Commonweal 88:289-291, May 24, 1968. F-31

Fichter, Joseph H. That celibacy survey, America
116:92-94, Jan. 21, 1967. F-32

First exclusive survey of non-hospital abortions.
Lader, Lawrence, Look 33:63-65, Jan. 21, 1969. F-33

First notifications. Economist 229:50, Nov. 2,
1968. F-34

First year of the abortion act. Abels, S., Lancet,
1:1051-1052, May 24, 1969. F-35

Fleck, J. C. Canada debates abortion, homosexuality, Christian Century 86:354-358, Mar. 12,
1969. F-36

Fletcher, Joseph. Interview, St. Louis-Post-Dis-
patch, Dec. 15, 1969. F-37

Fletcher, Joseph. Situation Ethics. Westminster
Press, 1966. F-38

Flood, Peter. The Abortion Act 1967, Clergy Review 53:42-48, Jan. 1968. F-39

Flood, Peter. New Problems in Medical Ethics
#4 S.V.D. Techny, Ill., 1963. F-40

Focus on Hope. Box 7337, Milwaukee, Wisc.,
53213. Lenten series on morality. F-41

Forced Birth Control. Social Justice Review 62:
273, Dec. 1969. F-42

Ford, S. Homosexuals and the law, Calif.

Western Law Review 5:232-240, Spring 1969.            F-43

Forgue, Joseph.   Sexuality on the island earth,
    Ecumenist 7:81-87,   Sept. 1969.                 F-44

Fort, Joel.   Drug use and the law, Current 113:
    4-13, Dec. 1969.                                 F-45

Francis, Dale.   The plot to kill my son, Catholic
    Digest 31:20-22, Apr. 1967.                      F-46

Francoeur, Robert.   And baby makes one, Critic
    28:34-41, Nov. 1969.                             F-47

Frank, Stanley.   Sexually active man past forty,
    Macmillan, 1968.                                 F-48

Freedman, Ronald.   Family Planning in Taiwan,
    Princeton University Press, 1969.                F-49

Freeland, William.   Inter-faith debate on easing
    abortion laws, Christianity Today 11:43, Apr.
    28, 1967.                                        F-50

Frein, George.   Celibacy: the Necessary Option,
    Herder and Herder, 1968.                         F-51

Friedenberg, Edgar.   Dignity of Youth and Other
    Atavisms, Beacon, 1969.                          F-52

Frisbie, Richard.   Six Paradoxes of Sex, Claretian
    Press, 1969.                                     F-53

Frisbie, Richard.   Six paradoxes of sex, U. S.
    Catholic 34:12-18, Nov. 1968.                    F-54

Fryer, Peter.   Birth controllers, Secker & War-
    burg, 1965.                                      F-55

Fundamental right.   Scientific American 221:56-57,
    Nov. 1969.                                       F-56

Furstenberg, Frank.   Birth control knowledge and
    attitudes among unmarried pregnant adolescents,
    Journal of Marriage and the Family 31: 34-42,
    Feb. 1969.                                       F-57

Gagern, Frederick von. New Views on Sex, Marriage, Love, Paulist Press, 1968.　　G-1

Gagnon, John. Psychosexual development, Trans-Action 6:9-17, Mar. 1969.　　G-2

Gallagher, Ursula. Effective Patterns of Services to Unmarried Parents, Health, Education and Welfare Dept. 1968.　　G-3

Gallagher, Ursula. National Trends in Services to Unmarried Parents, Health, Education and Welfare Dept. 1968.　　G-4

Ganguli, H. Family planning situation in India, Indian Journal of Social Work 29:233-239, 1969.　　G-5

Gay World. Hoffman, Martin, Basic Books, 1968.　　G-6

Gebhard, Paul. Sex Offenders, Harper, 1965.　　G-7

George, B. Current abortion laws, Western Reserve Press, 1967.　　G-8

Gerharz, George. Birth regulation and situation ethics, Listening 3:208-213, Autumn 1968.　　G-9

Gest, John. Comments, Catholic Lawyer 14:326-328, Fall 1968.　　G-10

Gest, John. Proposed abortion laws: slaughter of the innocents, Linacre Quarterly 36:47-52, Feb. 1969.　　G-11

Ghorbani, F.S. Birth control and population, Medical Gynaecology and Sociology 4:228-233, Sept. 1969.　　G-12

47

Giannella, Donald.   Difficult quest, <u>Villanova Law</u>
<u>Review</u> 13:297-269, Winter 1968.                    G-13

Girard, Alain.   Public survey on family structure
and birth control.   <u>Sociological Abstracts</u> 17:7,
#E0647, Dec. 1969.                                       G-14

Glock, Charles.   <u>Prejudice U.S.A.</u>, Praeger, 1969.   G-15

<u>God, Sex and Youth</u>.   Hulme, William, Concordia,
1968.                                                    G-16

Gonzalez, Gerardo.   Birth control in Chile, <u>Cath</u>-
<u>olic Mind</u> 113:29-34, Dec. 1969.                        G-17

Goodman, Irv.   The bedroom should not be within
the province of the law, <u>Calif. Western Law Re</u>-
<u>view</u> 4:115-131, Spring 1968.                           G-18

Goodrich, T.   The morality of killing, <u>Philosophy</u>
44, #130, Oct. 1969.                                     G-19

Gordis, Robert.   <u>Sex and the Family in Jewish</u>
<u>Tradition</u>.   Burning Bush Press, 1967.                G-20

Gordon, Arthur.   Louisiana's quiet revolution in
family planning, <u>Today's Health</u> 40:38-41, Jan.
1970.                                                    G-21

Gorkin, A.   Concern for the Soviet family, <u>The</u>
<u>Soviet Review</u> 10:47-53, Fall 1969.                     G-22

Gough, C.   Abortion, <u>Modern Churchman</u> 10:231-
235, Apr. 1967.                                          G-23

Gould, Donald.   Abortion in perspective, <u>New States</u>-
<u>man</u> 78:42-43, July 11, 1969.                          G-24

Gould, Donald.   Crossman and the pill, <u>New States</u>-
<u>man</u> 77:686-687, May 16, 1969.                         G-25

Gould, Donald.   Snags of legal abortion, <u>New States</u>-
<u>man</u> 75:543-544, Apr. 26, 1968.                        G-26

Gould, Donald.   Test-tube question, <u>New Statesman</u>
77:251-252, Feb. 21, 1969.                              G-27
48

Gould, Robert.  Understanding homosexuality, _Seventeen_ 28:90-91, July 1969.                        G-28

Government and the copulation explosion.  Rice, Charles, _Triumph_ 4:16-19, Mar. 1969.              G-29

Granfield, David.  _The Abortion Decision_, Doubleday, 1969.                                         G-30

_Great Issues of Conscience in Modern Medicine_. Dartmouth Convocation, Hanover, Sept. 8 - 10, 1960.                                                G-31

Greeley, Andrew.  _Strangers in the House_.  Rev. ed., Doubleday, 1967.                              G-32

Greeley, Andrew.  We can't walk alone, _Sign_ 48: 20-23, May 1969.                                   G-33

Green, Ronald.  Abortion and promise-keeping, _Christianity in Crisis_ 27:109-113, May 15, 1967 195-196, Aug. 7; 220-222, Oct. 2.             G-34

Grisez, Germain.  Abortion and the Catholic Faith, _American Ecclesiastical Review_ 159:96-115, Aug. 1968.                                            G-35

Grisez, Germain.  New formulation of a natural law argument against contraception, _Thomist_ 30: 343-361, Oct. 1966.                              G-36

Group approach to young unwed mothers.  Barclay, Lillian, _Social Casework_ 50:379-384, July 1969.   G-37

Group for the Advancement of Pyschiatry.  _The Right to Abortion_, GAP 7, #75, Oct. 1969.           G-38

Group for the Advancement of Psychiatry.  _Sex and the College Student_, G.A.P. Report, Vol. VI, #60, Nov. 1965.                                    G-39

Growing battle over abortion reform.  Maisel, Albert, _Readers Digest_ 94:152-154, June 1969.       G-40

_Growing up in a Philippine Barrio_.  Jocano, F.,

49

Holt, Rinehart and Winston, 1969.                    G-41

Growing Up Straight. Wyden, Peter, Stein and Day,
1968.                                                G-42

Guideline on abortion. Time 94:66, Sept. 19, 1969.   G-43

Gustafson, James. Christian approach to the ethics
of abortion, Dublin Review 241:346-364, Winter
1967.                                                G-44

Gustafson, James. Protestant response (to Darst-
Forgue) Ecumenist 7:87-89, Sept. 1969.              G-45

Guttmacher, Alan. Birth Control and Love, Macmillan, 1969.                                        G-46

Guttmacher, Alan. The Case for Legalized Abortion
Now. Diablo Press, 1967.                             G-47

Guttmacher, Alan. Family planning; needs and
methods, American Journal of Nursing 69:1229-
1234, June 1969.                                     G-48

Guttmacher, Alan. How to succeed at family planning, Parents Magazine 44:54-55, Jan. 1969.         G-49

Guttmacher, Alan. When pregnancy means heartbreak, McCalls 95:60-61, Apr. 1968.                 G-50

Hall, R.   Therapeutic abortion, sterilization and
contraception, American Journal of Obstetrics
and Gynecology 91:581-585, 1965.                     H-1

Hall, Robert.   Child, his birth without permission,
Saturday Review 52:59-60, Mar. 1, 1969.             H-2

Hardin, Garrett.   Abortion--or compulsory pregnancy, Journal of Marriage and the Family 30:
246-251, May 1968.                                   H-3

Hardin, Garrett.   Blueprints, D. N. A. and abortion, Medical Opinion and Review, 1967.             H-4

Hardin, Garrett.   Population, Evolution and Birth
Control, Freeman, (2nd ed.) 1969.                    H-5

Hardin, Garrett.   Science and Controversy, Freeman, 1969.                                           H-6

Harrington, Charles.   Sexual differentiation in
socializations and some male genital mutilations,
American Anthropologist 70:951-956, Oct. 1968.       H-7

Harrington, Michael.   The betrayal of the poor,
Atlantic 225:71-74, Jan. 1970.                       H-8

Harrington, Paul,   Abortion, Linacre Quarterly,
1969 issues.                                         H-9

Harrington, Paul.   Abortion: Japan, Linacre
Quarterly 36:139-143 May, 1969.                      H-10

Harrington, Paul.   Is abortion a crime?  Family
Digest 23:7-13, Jan. 1968.                           H-11

Harrington, Timothy.   Legalization of abortion,

Homiletic and Pastoral Review 69:685-690, June
1969.                                              H-12

Harris, Alan.  Battle against ignorance, superstition and moralizing, New Statesman 77:284-
287, Feb. 28, 1969.                                H-13

Harris, Sara.  The Puritan Jungle, Putnam, 1969.   H-14

Harvard Divinity School.  International Conference
on Abortion, Proceedings, 1967.                    H-15

Harvey, John.  Female Homosexuality, Linacre
Quarterly 36:100-106, May 1969.                    H-16

Hathaway, Alden.  Sex education in the Church,
Pastoral Psychology 19:7-14, May 1968.             H-17

Hay, Gerald.  Apologia pro Vita Humana, Homiletic
and Pastoral Review 70:283-286, Jan. 1970.         H-18

Hayes, Thomas.  Abortion, Commonweal 85:686-
679, Mar. 17, 1967.                                H-19

Hayes, Thomas.  Biology of the reproductive act,
Insight 6:12-19, Fall 1967.                        H-20

Health, Education and Welfare Department.  Family
Planning: Nationwide Opportunities, U. S. Govt.
Pub. 1968,  FS1. 2:F21/2/968.                      H-21

Heerin, Henk.  Family planning and differential
fertility, Journal of Marriage and the Family
31:588-595, Aug. 1969.                             H-22

Hellegers, Andre.  Abortion, the law and the
common good, Catholic Mind 65:28-39, Dec.,
1967.                                              H-23

Heller, A. Colorado story, American Journal of
Psychiatry 125:809-816, 1968.                      H-24

Hellman, Louis.  The pill: a second look, FDA
Papers 3:8, Oct. 1969.                             H-25

Heltsley, Mary. Religiosity and premarital sexual
  permissiveness, Journal of Marriage and the
  Family 31:441-445, Aug. 1969.                    H-26
Hennessy, Augustine. Debate on legalized abor-
  tion, Sign 46:34-35, June 1967.                  H-27
Hentoff, Margot. Abortion, Jubilee 14:4-5, Apr.
  1967.                                            H-27a
Hibbard, L. Abortion, gas embolus and sudden
  death, California Medicine 110:305-308, Apr.
  1969.                                            H-28
Hidden World of the Sex Offenders, Parker, Tony,
  Bobbs, 1969.                                     H-29
High court test of abortion law. National Catholic
  Reporter 6:3, Jan. 14, 1970.                     H-30
Hill, Reuben. Research on human fertility, Inter-
  national Social Science Journal 226-228, 1968.   H-31
Hill, Reuben. Social aspects of family planning,
  World Justice 9:167-173, Dec. 1967.             H-32
Hindell, Keith. How the abortion lobby worked,
  Political Quarterly 39:268-282, July 1968.      H-33
Hinds, Illene. Welfare mother, Christian Century
  87:17-18, Jan. 7, 1970.                          H-34
Hirschhorn, Kurt. On re-doing man, Commonweal
  86:257-261, May 17, 1968.                        H-35
History of abortion and the Church. Noonan, John,
  Theology Digest 16:251-258, Autumn 1968.        H-36
History of Contraceptives. Suitters, Beryl, Lon-
  don, International Planned Parenthood, 1967.     H-37
Hitchcock, James. Sex, Church and culture,
  Catholic World 209:17-20, Apr. 1969             H-38
Hoagland, H. Control of fertility, Science 161:
  1261, Sept. 20, 1968.                            H-39

Hoffman, Martin.  The Gay World.  Basic Books,
    1968.                                                       H-40

Hoffman, Paul.  A Time to Plan, a Time to Work,
    United Nations Pub. 1969 DP/L 108.          H-41

Homosexual role.  McIntosh, Mary, Social Problems
    16:182-192, Fall 1968.                        H-42

Homosexuality in the Bible and the law.  Smith,
    B., Christianity Today 13:7-10, July 18, 1969.    H-43

Homosexuals and the law.  Ford, S., California
    Western Law Review 5:232-240, Spring 1969.    H-44

Honest Sex.  Roy, Rustum, New American Li-
    brary, 1968.                                     H-45

Hostage Seekers.  Humphrey, Michael, Humanities
    Press, 1969.                                   H-46

Hottel, Althea, ed.  Women Around the World.
    Annals of the American Academy of Political and
    Social Science 375-385 Jan. 1968.           H-47

Hough, Joseph.  Rules and the ethics of sex, Chris-
    tian Century 86:148-151, Jan. 29, 1969.       H-48

Hoult, Thomas.  Dictionary of Modern Sociology,
    Little, Adam, 1969.                          H-49

House Divided.  Melady, Thomas, Sheed and Ward,
    1969.                                          H-50

How California's abortion law isn't working.  Monroe,
    Keith, New York Times Magazine, Dec. 29,
    1968 pp 10-11; comment, Jan. 12, 1969, p. 6.    H-51

How deep will the government get into birth control?
    Shaw, Russell, Columbia 50:6, Jan. 1970.     H-52

How the abortion lobby worked.  Hindell, Keith,
    Political Quarterly 39:268-282, July 1968.     H-53

How to succeed at family planning.  Guttmacher,
    Alan, Parents Magazine 44:54-55, Jan. 1969.   H-54

Howard, Marion. School Continues for Pregnant
Teenagers, U. S. Govt. Pub. 1969, FS5. 220:
20115.                                                                   H-55

Hoyman, H. Our most explosive sex education
issue, Journal of School Health 39:458-469 Sept.
1969.                                                                    H-56

Hoyman, H. Should we teach about birth control
in high school? Education Digest 34:20-23,
Feb. 1969.                                                               H-57

Hoyt, Robert. Abortion issues clouded, National
Catholic Reporter, 3:1, Sept. 13, 1967.                                  H-58

Hoyt, Robert. Afterthoughts, National Catholic Re-
porter 3:10, Sept. 20, 1967.                                             H-59

Hoyt, Robert. Birth Control Debate, National
Catholic Reporter, 1968.                                                 H-60
No entry                                                                 H-61

Hughes, Douglas. Perspectives on Pornography,
St. Martin's, 1970.                                                      H-62

Hugo, John. St. Augustine on Nature, Sex, and
Marriage, Scepter 1969.                                                  H-63

Huldt, L. Outcome of pregnancy when legal abor-
tion is readily available, Lancet 1:467,1968.                            H-64

Hulka, J. Mathematical model study of contraceptive efficiency and unwanted pregnancies,
American Journal of Obstetrics and Gynecology,
104:443-447, June 1, 1969.                                               H-65

Hulme, William. God, Sex and Youth, Concordia,
1968.                                                                    H-66

Human Guinea Pigs. Pappworth, M. H. , Beacon,
1968.                                                                    H-66a

Human Mystery of Sexuality. Oraison, Marc, Sheed
and Ward 1967.                                                           H-67

55

Human Sexual Response. Masters, W., and John-
son, V., Saunders, 1966.                                    H-68

Human sexuality in a time of change. Callahan,
Sidney Christian Century 85:1077-1080, Aug.
28, 1968: 1310, Oct. 16, 1968.                              H-69

Human Sexuality. McCary, James, Van Nostrand,
1967.                                                       H-70

Humanae Vitae. Pamphlet editions from Paulist
Press, St. Paul Editions and U.S. Catholic
Conference.                                                 H-71

Humane doctors; inhumane law. Nation 206:261,
Feb. 26, 1968.                                              H-72

Humane stand on abortion. Markham, Rosemary,
Catholic Charities Review 51:4-6, Apr. 1967.                H-73

Humanizing the abortion debate. Diamond, James,
America 121:36-39, July 19, 1969.                           H-74

Humphrey, Michael. The Hostage Seekers, Human-
ities Press, 1969.                                          H-75

Hunt, John. Responsibility of Dissent, Sheed &
Ward, 1970.                                                 H-76

Hunt, William. Theologian challenges Fr.
Drinan, National Catholic Reporter 4:6, Jan.
19, 1968.                                                   H-77

Huser, Roger. Crime of Abortion in Canon Law,
Catholic University Press, 1942.                            H-78

Jesuit denies abortion in early stages is immoral.
Andrews, James, National Catholic Reporter 5:6,
Nov. 27, 1968.                                                J-1

Jewett, Paul.   Relation of the soul to the fetus,
Christianity Today 13:6-9, Nov. 8, 1968.                      J-2

Jewish and gentile norms.   Fathi, Asghar, Phylon
29:5-12, Spring 1968.                                         J-3

Jocano, F.   Growing up in a Philippine barrio,
Holt, Rinehart and Winston, 1969.                             J-4

Johnson, Harvey.   Is embryonic life human?
Social Justice Review 59:431-432, Mar. 1967.                  J-5

Jones, Gavin.   Use of oral contraceptives, Studies
in Family Planning 24:1-13, Dec. 1967.                        J-6

Joyce, R.   Unborn children defined outside humanity, Arizona Register 46:6-7, Jan. 2, 1970.                   J-7

Justifiable abortion.   Quay, Eugene, Georgetown
Law Journal 49:156-173, Winter 1960; 395-538,
Spring 1961.                                                  J-8

Kalman, S.  Effects of oral contraceptives, <u>Annual</u>
<u>Review of Pharmacology</u> 9:363-378, 1969.                    K-1

Karlen, Arno.  Unmarried couples on campus, <u>New</u>
<u>York Times Magazine</u> 28-29, Jan. 1969; discussion,
p. 16, Feb. 16, Feb. 23, 1969.                                      K-2

Kaufman, S.  Impact of infertility, <u>Fertility-Ster-</u>
<u>ility</u> 20:380-383, May 1969.                                   K-3

Kelleher, Stephen.  The intolerable marriage,
<u>America</u> 119+178-182, Sept. 14, 1968; 434-
436, Nov. 9, 1968.                                                  K-4

Kennedy, Eugene.  Sexuality.  <u>Critic</u> 27:26-31,
June 1969.                                                          K-5

Kennedy, Jeremiah.  Debate on legalized abortion,
<u>Sign</u> 46:34-35, June 1967.                                    K-6

<u>Key to Feminine Response in Marriage</u>.  Deutsche,
Ronald, Random, 1968.                                               K-7

Kiell, Norman.  <u>Universal Experience of Adol-</u>
<u>escence</u>, Beacon, 1969.                                        K-7a

Kindregan, Charles.  <u>Theology of Marriage</u>, Bruce,
1967.                                                               K-8

King of the abortionists.  Spencer, Robert, <u>News-</u>
<u>week</u> 73:92, Feb. 17, 1969.                                    K-9

Kinsey in Russian.  <u>Current Abstracts of the Soviet</u>
<u>Press</u>, 1:(8)11-12, Jan. 1969.                                K-10

Kirkendall, Lester.  Is sexual freedom a mirage?
<u>Marriage</u> 51:64-70, June 1969; 51-58, July 1969.     K-11

Kiser, Clyde.  Trends and Variations in Fertility in the United States, Harvard University Press, 1968.                                                    K-12

Kistner, Robert.  The Pill: Facts and Fallacies, Delacorte, 1969.                                    K-13

Klein, Isaac.  Abortion: a Jewish view, Dublin Review 241:382-390, Winter 1967.                K-14

Klein, John.  Pilgrims progress: recent developments in family theory, Journal of Marriage and the Family 32:677-687, Nov. 1969.          K-15

Knight, Jill.  Right to be born, Tablet 221:285-286, Mar. 18, 1967.                                   K-16

Kogler, James.  Crisis of Morality, Focus on Hope, 1970.                                              K-17

Koontz, E.  Teen-agers speak out, Today's Education 58:23-26, Mar. 1969.                    K-18

Kovacs, L.  One hundred therapeutic abortions, Medical Gynaecology and Sociology 4:142-145, June 1969.                                    K-19

Kraditor, Aileen.  Up from Pedestal, Quadrangle, 1968.                                              K-20

Kramer, Herbert.  Abortion, who should decide? Liguorian 56:33-36, Jan. 1968.              K-21

Krause, James.  Is abortion absolutely prohibited? Continuum 6:436-440, Fall 1968.          K-22

Kremer, M.  Early development of homosexuality, American Journal of Psychiatry 126:91-96, July 1969.                                          K-23

Kronhausen, Phyllis.  Erotic Fantasies, Grove, 1970.                                              K-24

Kucera, E.  Fertility after operations of extra-uterine pregnancies, International Journal of

_Fertility_ 14:127-129, Apr. 1969.       K-25

Kummer, Jerome. _Abortion: Legal and Illegal_,
    author, Santa Monica, Cal., 1967.       K-26

Kutner, Luis. Due process of abortion, _Min-
    nesota Law Review_ 53:1-10, Nov. 1968.       K-27

Kuttner, Robert. Red and green in civil rights.
    _Commonweal_ 90:535, Sept. 5, 1969.       K-28

Lader, Lawrence.   Abortion, Bobbs-Merrill,
  1966.                                                          L-1

Lader, Lawrence.   First exclusive survey of
  non-hospital abortions, Look 33:63-65, Jan.
  21, 1969.                                                      L-2

Lader, Lawrence.   Mothers who chose abortions,
  Redbook 130-8, Feb. 1968.                                     L-3

Lader, Lawrence.   New abortion laws, Parents
  Magazine 43:48-49, Apr. 1968.                                 L-4

Lader, Lawrence.   Who has the right to live?
  Good Housekeeping 166:84-85, June 1968.                       L-5

Lader, Lawrence.   Why birth control fails, Mc-
  Calls, 97-5, Oct. 1969.                                       L-6

Language, taboo and human uniqueness.   Wescott,
  Roger, Bucknell Review 17:28-37, Dec. 1969.                   L-7

Latin American Development.   Weaver, Jerry,
  American Bibliographical Center, 1969.                        L-8

Lauth, Edward.   The antithesis of the practice
  of medicine, Catholic Mind 66:20-27, Mar.
  1968.                                                          L-9

Lauth, Edward.   Liberal abortion laws, Linacre
  Quarterly 34:367-373, Nov. 1967.                              L-10

Lavelle, Joseph.   Is abortion good medicine?   Linacre Quarterly 35:16-23, Feb. 1968.                           L-11

Law, morality and abortion.   Rutgers Law Re-
  view 22:415-420, Spring 1968.                                 L-12

Law of New York on abortion.  Means, Cyril,
New York Law Forum 14:411-415, Fall 1968.      L-13

Lawler, Justus.  Professor Grisez and natural
law, New Blackfriars 48:250-255, Feb. 1967.     L-14

Laws Governing Family Planning.  Weinberg, Roy,
Oceana, 1968.                                   L-15

Leavy, Zad.  California's new therapeutic abortion
act, UCLA Law Review 15:1-31, Nov. 1967.        L-16

Leavy, Zad.  Therapeutic abortion act of 1967,
Los Angeles Bar Bulletin 43:111-115, Jan. 1968.  L-17

Lee, Nancy.  The Search for an Abortionist.
University of Chicago press, 1969.              L-18

Legal abortions.  Christianity Today 14:43, Nov.
21, 1969.                                       L-19

Legal abortions: an unholy mess in Britain.  Carlova, John, Medical Economics 270-289, Oct.
13, 1969.                                       L-20

Legal abortion in Eastern Europe.  Potts, Malcolm, Eugenics Review 59:232-250, Dec. 1967.    L-21

Legal aspects of abortion.  New York Bar Association Record 22:118-123, Feb. 1967.           L-22

Legalization of abortion.  Harrington, Timothy,
Homiletic and Pastoral Review 69:685-690,
June 1969.                                      L-23

Legalized abortion.  Hospital Progress 49:16,
Jan. 1968.                                      L-24

Legalized abortion.  Lynch, John, Linacre
Quarterly 35:38-41, Feb. 1968.                  L-25

Legman, G.  Oragenitalism, Julian Press, 1969.  L-26

Leinwald, Gerald.  Poverty and the Poor.  Washington Square Press, 1968.                      L-27

Lelys, David.  Research and adolescent habits,

Pastoral Life 18:18-21, Nov. 1969.                    L-28

Leo, John.  Reaching a consensus on abortion,
  National Catholic Reporter 3:11, Feb. 8, 1967.     L-29

Leo, John.  Why control births with a knife?
  National Catholic Reporter 3:8, Feb. 22, 1967.     L-30

Leonard, George.  The Man and Woman Thing.
  Delacorte 1970.                                     L-31

Lesser of two evils.  Tablet, Feb.-June 1966.        L-32

Let's think about abortion.  Schenk, Roy, Catholic World 207:15-17, Apr. 1968.                   L-33

Level of sexual experience.  Shope, David, Journal
  of Marriage and the Family 29:424-433, Aug.
  1967.                                               L-34

Lewit, Sarah.  Abortion.  Scientific American
  220:21-27, Jan. 1969.                              L-35

Lewontin, Richard.  Population, Biology and Evolution, Syracuse University Press, 1968.           L-36

Liberal abortion laws.  Ayd, Frank, America 120:
  130-132, Feb. 1, 1969.                             L-37

Liberal abortion laws.  Ayd, Frank, American
  Ecclesiastical Review 158:73-91, Feb. 1968.        L-38

Liberal abortion laws.  Ayd, Frank, Marriage 51:
  40-43, June 1969.                                  L-39

Liberal abortion laws.  Lauth, Edward, Linacre
  Quarterly 34:367-373, Nov. 1967.                   L-40

Life before birth.  Montagu, Ashley, New American Library 1965.                                 L-41

Limner, Roman.  Sex and the Unborn Child, Julian,
  1969.                                               L-42

Lister, J.  Unwanted pregnancy, New England
  Journal of Medicine 280:1463-1465, June 26, 1969. L-43

Liu, William.  Catholics U.S.A., Wiley, 1970.        L-44

Lively Debate. Shannon, William, Sheed and
   Ward, 1969.                                            L-45

Living with the Pill. Baird, Douglas, London,
   Times Newspapers, 1969.                                L-46

Lord, to whom shall we go? Worden, Thomas,
   Concilium, Vol. 50, 121-138.                           L-47

Loreusen, Willard.   Abortion and the crime-sin
   spectrum, West Virginia Law Review 70:20-25,
   Dec. 1967.                                             L-48

Louisell, David.   Abortion, medicine and due process, UCLA Law Review 16:233-240, Feb. 1969.   L-49

Louisell, David.   Father as non-parent, Catholic
   World 210:108-110, Dec. 1969.                          L-49a

Louisiana's quiet revolution in family planning.
   Gordon, Arthur, Today's Health 40:38-41, Jan.
   1970.                                                  L-50

Love and Sexuality. Ryan, Mary Perkins, Holt,
   1967.                                                  L-51

Love and the Married Woman. Chesser, Eustace,
   Putnam, 1969.                                          L-52

Love in the Western World. Crewes, Frederick,
   Partisan Review 34:272-287, Spring 1967.              L-53

Lunneborg, Patricia.   Sex differences in aptitude
   maturation during college, Journal of Counseling
   Psychology 16:463-464, Sept. 1969.                     L-54

Lynch, John.   Legalized abortion, Linacre Quarterly 35:38-41, Feb. 1968.                            L-55

Lyons, Bernard.   Abortion's crucial question, Extension 62:17-21, Oct. 1967.                           L-56

McCalister, Donald. Family planning and the reduction of pregnancy loss rate, Journal of Marriage and the Family 31:668-673, Nov. 1969.  M-1

McCary, James. Human Sexuality, Van Nostrand, 1967.  M-2

McCleave, P. On view: on therapeutic abortion, Journal of the Iowa Medical Society 59:195-197, Mar. 1969.  M-3

McCormick, Richard. Aspects of the moral question, America 117:716-719, Dec. 9, 1967.  M-4

McCormick, Richard. Christian morals, America 122:5-6, Jan. 10, 1970.  M-5

McCormick, Richard. Conference without consensus, America 117:716-719, Sept. 23, 1967.  M-6

McCormick, Richard. Current Theology, Jan.-June 1969, Theological Studies 30:635-692, Dec. 1969.  M-7

McCormick, Richard. Magisterium and contraception, Theological Studies 19:707-735, Dec. 1968.  M-8

McCormick, Richard. Past Church teaching on abortion, Proceedings, American Catholic Philosophical Association, 23:131-151, 1968.  M-9

McCready, Robert. Our Bed Is Flourishing, Sheed & Ward, 1969.  M-10

McCully, H. Pliny's pheromonic abortifacients, Science 165:236-237, July 18, 1969.  M-11

McDonagh, Michael. Ethical problems of abortion, Irish Theological Quarterly 35:268-297,

67

July 1968. M-12

McGrath, P. Natural law, Homiletic and Pastoral Review 69:112-122, Nov. 1968. M-13

Machina ex Deo. White, Lynn, MIT Press, 1969. M-14

McHugh, James. Report on the International Conference on Abortion, American Ecclesiastical Review 157: 328-332, Nov. 1967. M-15

McHugh, James. Statement on sex education, Bulletin of the Guild of Catholic Psychiatrists 15: 143-146, July 1968. M-16

McIntosh, Mary. The homosexual role, Social Problems 16:182-192, Fall 1968. M-17

McKerron, Jane. Abortion backlash, New Statesman 78:5-6, July 4, 1969. M-18

McKerron, Jane. Abortion: can doctors cope? New Statesman 75:166, Feb. 9, 1968. M-19

McLaughlin, John. Abortion and the law, St. Anthony's Messenger 76:51-55, Nov. 1968. M-20

McLaughlin, John. Christian re-examination of sex, St. Anthony's Messenger, articles, Apr.- Aug. 1968, Jan. and Apr. 1969. M-21

McLaughlin, John. Education in human sexuality, America 121:494-497, Nov. 22, 1969. M-22

McLaughlin, John. Education in sex education, Catholic School Journal 69:16-18, Oct. 1969. M-23

McNally, Arthur. Debate on legalized abortion, Sign 46:35, June 1967. M-24

McNamara, Robert. Organizations, colleges and values, Sociological Analysis 30:125-131, Fall 1969. M-25

Magisterium and contraception. McCormick, Richard, Theological Studies 29:707-735, Dec. 1968. M-26

68

Maisel, Albert.   Growing battle over abortion re-
    form, Readers Digest 94:152-154, June 1969.        M-27
Making men and women without people.   Rorvik,
    David, Esquire, Apr. 1969, pp. 108-115.            M-28
Male and female: Fact and Fiction.   Steinman,
    Ann, Denver, Colo., Loretto Heights College,
    1969, 16p. $1.15.                                  M-29
Male-female relations in Europe.   Catholic World
    210:64-69, Nov. 1969.                              M-30
Male-oriented fertility control experiment.   Peel,
    J., Practitioner 202:677-681, May, 1969.           M-31
Malo, T.   Hazards of plastic bell circumcisions,
    Obstetrics and Gynecology 33:869, June 1969.       M-32
Man and the Woman.   Evoy, John, Sheed and
    Ward, 1969.                                        M-33
Man and woman.   Stern, Karl, Catholic Digest 33:
    90-93, Apr. 1969.                                  M-34
Man and Woman Thing.   Leonard, George, Dela-
    corte, 1970.                                       M-35
Man of Tomorrow.   Delaunay, Albert, Doubleday,
    1966.                                              M-36
Man plays God.   Linacre Quarterly 35:42, Jan.
    1969.                                              M-37
Man's vengeance on woman, Moody, Howard, Renewal
    7:6-8, Feb. 1967.                                  M-38
Manual of clinical contraception.   Bill, H., North
    Carolina Medical Journal 30:169-182, May 1969.     M-39
Markham, Rosemary.   A humane stand on abortion,
    Catholic Charities Review 51:4-6, Apr. 1967.       M-40
Marr, Susan.   Abortion à la suisse, New States-
    man 73: Apr. 7, 1967.                              M-41
Marriage and Family Counseling.   Peterson, James,
69

Association, 1968.     M-42

Marriage: Before and After.   Popenoe, Paul, American Institute of Family Relations (Los Angeles)
1969.     M-43

Marriage: Human Reality and Saving Mystery.
Schillesbeeckx, Edward, Sheed and Ward, 1966.   M-44

Marriage is What You Make It.   Popenoe, Paul,
American Institute of Family Relations (Los
Angeles) 1969.     M-45

Marriage: Psychological and Moral Approach, Bier,
William, Fordham University Press, 1969.   M-46

Married couples must decide for themselves.   Tablet
221:447, Apr. 22, 1967.     M-47

Masters, W. H., and V. E. Johnson.   Human Sexual
Response, Saunders, 1966.     M-48

Masters, W. H. Interview.   Playboy, May 1969.   M-49

Masturbation: an objectively grave matter.   Curran,
Charles E., Proceedings, Catholic Theological
Society of America 21:95-109, 1966.     M-50

Maternal deaths with septic shock after criminal
abortion.   Ohio Medical Journal 65:601-603,
June 1969.     M-51

Mathematical model study of contraceptive efficiency
and unwanted pregnancies.   Hulka, J., American
Journal of Obstetrics and Gynecology 104:443-447,
June 1, 1969.     M-52

Matter of life and death.   Schick, Tom, St. Anthony's
Messenger 77:36-37, Aug. 1969.     M-53

Mayhew, Leonard.   Abortion: two sides, Ecumenist
5:75-77, July 1967.     M-54

Maynard, Rona.   In my opinion, Seventeen 28:228,
Feb. 1969.     M-55

Mazur, Ronald.  Common Sense Sex, Beacon Press,
    1968.                                         M-56

Mead, Margaret.  Culture and Commitment, Double-
    day 1969.                                      M-57

Mead, Margaret.  A Way of Seeing, McCalls,
    1970.                                        M-58

Means, Cyril.  Law of New York on abortion,
    New York Law Forum 14:411-415, Fall 1968.    M-59

Medical-Moral Newsletter.  Abortion as birth
    control, Jan. 1967, vol. 3#5, 912 W. Lake Ave.,
    Baltimore, Md. 21210.                  M-60

Medical moral problems in a troubled society.
    Ayd, Frank, NCEA Bulletin 66:97-102, Aug. 1969.  M-61

Melady, Thomas.  House Divided, Sheed and Ward,
    1970.                                        M-62

MP's act on abortion.  Tablet 221-541, May 13,
    1967.                                        M-63

Meyerowitz, S.  Who may not have an abortion?
    Journal of the American Medical Association,
    209:260-261, July, 1969.                M-64

Michelmore, Susan.  Sexual Reproduction, Natural
    History Press, Doubleday, 1964.         M-65

Micklin, Michael.  Urban life and differential fer-
    tility, Sociological Quarterly 10:480-500, Fall,
    1969.                                        M-66

Minority's plea.  Alverson, Charles, Wall Street
    Journal 172:1, July 17, 1968.            M-67

Mintz, Morton.  By Prescription Only, Beacon,
    1969.                                        M-68

Mintz, Morton.  The Pill. Beacon, 1970.      M-68a

Money, J. Psychosexual developments, Journal
    of Nervous and Mental Disorders 148:111-123,

Feb. 1969.                                                          M-69

Monroe, Keith.   How California's abortion law isn't
    working, New York Times Magazine Dec. 26,
    1968, pp. 10-11; replies Jan. 12, 1969, p. 6.              M-70

Montagu, see Ashley-Montagu, M. A.                             M-71

Montserrat-Torrents, Jose.   The Abandoned
    Spouse.   Bruce 1969.                                      M-72

Moody, Howard.   Man's vengeance on woman,
    Renewal 7:6-8, Feb. 1967.                                  M-73

Moore, Marcena.   Sex, sex, sex.   Pilgrim Press,
    1969.                                                      M-74

Morality of abortion laws, Drinan, Robert, Cath-
    olic Lawyer 14:190-198, Summer 1968.                       M-75

Morality of killing.   Goodrich, T., Philosophy 44:
    #130, Oct. 1969.                                           M-76

Morality today.   Cross, Wilford, Churchman 184:
    6-7, Jan. 1970.                                            M-77

Morals, Law and Life.   Daly, Cahal, Scepter, 1966.           M-78

Morriss, Frank.   Abortion compromise and ecu-
    menism, Social Justice Review 60:264-265, Dec.
    1967.                                                      M-79

Mosh, Stanley.  Population explosion and due process,
    Lincoln Law Review 1:149-165, June 1966.                  M-80

Moskin, J.   New contraceptive society, Look 33:
    50, Feb. 4, 1969.                                          M-81

Mothers who chose abortions.   Lader, Lawrence,
    Redbook 130:8-10, Feb. 1968.                              M-82

Moyer, C.   Delaware's abortion reform, Delaware
    Medical Journal 41:199, June 1969.                        M-83

Moynihan, Daniel.   On Fighting Poverty, Basic
    Books, 1969.                                              M-84

Moynihan, Daniel.   On Understanding Poverty,

Basic Books, 1969.                                      M-85

Mudd, Stuart.   Population Crisis and Use of
  World Resources, Indiana Univ.  Press, 1969.        M-86

Munson, H.   Abortion in modern times, Renewal
  7:9-10,  Feb.  1967.                                M-87

Murdoch, William.   All about ecology, Center
  Magazine,  3:56-63,  Jan.  1970.                    M-88

Murphy, Edmond.   Medical data and applied ethics,
  Linacre Quarterly 36:158-164, Aug.  1969.          M-89

Nagel, Thomas. Sexual perversion, <u>Journal of
Philosophy</u> 66:5-17, Jan. 16, 1969.        N-1

Naked American. Bentley, Eric, <u>New Republic</u>
161:31-34, Aug. 16, 1969.                     N-2

<u>Nameless: Abortion in Britain Today</u>. Ferris,
Paul, Hutchinson, 1966.                       N-3

Nathan, S. Pregnancies conceived extramaritally,
<u>Journal of the Royal College of General Practition-
ers</u> 18:72-81, Aug. 1969.                  N-4

National Catholic Reporter. <u>The Birth Control Debate,</u> National Catholic Reporter reprint, 1968.  N-5

National Commission on Human Life and Reproduction. Oak Park, Ill., <u>Newsletter</u>.  N-6

National Right to Life Committee. P.O. Box
9365, Washington, D.C., 20005, <u>Newsletter.</u>  N-7

<u>National Trends in Services to Unmarried Parents</u>.
Gallagher, Ursula, Health, Education and Welfare Dept. 1968.                              N-8

Natural Law argument. Conway, John, <u>Marriage</u>
49:44-49, May 1967.                           N-9

Natural law. McGrath, P., <u>Homiletic and Pastoral Review</u> 69:112-122, Nov. 1968.       N-10

<u>Never Ending Flower</u>. Younger, Susie, John Day,
1969.                                         N-11

New abortion laws. Lader, Lawrence, <u>Parents
Magazine</u> 43:48-49, Apr. 1968.            N-12

New abortion laws.  O'Donnell, Francis, <u>Bulletin</u>
of the Guild of Catholic Psychiatrists 15:91-93,
Apr. 1968.                                                   N-13

New contraceptive society.  Moskin, J., <u>Look</u>
33:50, Feb. 4, 1969.                                         N-14

New facts about human reproduction.  Ratcliff,
J., <u>Reader's Digest</u> 89:119-122, Dec. 1966.           N-15

New fashions in illegitimacy.  Illsley, Raymond,
<u>New Society</u> 12:709-711, Nov. 14, 1968.               N-16

New formulation of a natural law argument against
contraception.  Grusez, Germain, <u>Thomist</u> 30:
343-361, Oct. 1966.                                          N-17

<u>New Immorality</u>.  Walker, Brooks, Doubleday,
1969.                                                        N-18

New look at abortion.  Chandler, Russell, <u>Chris-</u>
<u>tianity Today</u> 11:28-30, Sept. 29, 1967.              N-19

The new North Carolina statute.  <u>North Carolina</u>
<u>Law Review</u> 46:585-590, Apr. 1968.                    N-20

<u>New Problems in Medical Ethics</u>.  #4.  S. V. D.
Publications, Techny, Ill., 1963.                            N-21

New theology of abortion reformers.  Byrn,
Robert, <u>Family Digest</u> 22:6-11, Feb. 1967.            N-22

<u>New Views on Sex, Marriage, Love</u>.  Von, Gagern,
Frederick, Paulist Press, 1968.                              N-23

New York abortion reform.  Caron, Wilfrid, <u>Cath-</u>
<u>olic Lawyer</u> 14:180-213, Summer, 1968.               N-24

New York Bar Association.  Legal aspects of
abortion, <u>Record</u> 22:118-123, Feb. 1967.             N-25

New York bishops pastoral.  <u>Catholic Mind</u> 65:5,
Apr. 1967.                                                   N-26

New York State.  <u>Report of the Governor's Com-</u>
<u>mission to Review the Abortion Law</u>.  Albany,

State of New York, Mar. 1968.                    N-27

New York State hearing: demonstration.  New
    Yorker 45:28-29, Feb. 22, 1969.              N-28

New York Times Index.  See entries under abor-
    tion, birth control, I.U.D., population, and
    research on contraceptives, etc.             N-29

Newsletter, Association for the Study of Abortion,
    120 W. 57th St., New York, N.Y., 10019.      N-30

Ng, Larry.  Population Crisis, Indiana University
    Press, 1969.                                 N-31

Noonan, John.  Abortion and the Catholic Church,
    Natural Law Forum 12:85-131, 1967.           N-32

Noonan, John.  Amendment of the abortion law,
    Catholic Lawyer 15:124-135, Spring 1969.     N-33

Noonan, John.  Authority, usury and contraception,
    Insight 6:29-42, Fall 1967.                  N-34

Noonan, John.  The Catholic Church and abortion,
    Dublin Review 241:300-345, Winter 1967.      N-35

Noonan, John.  Contraception, Harvard University
    Press, 1965.                                 N-36

Noonan, John.  History of abortion and the Church.
    Theology Digest 16:251-258, Autumn 1968.     N-37

Norwick, Kenneth.  When Should Abortion Be
    Legal?  N.Y. Public Affairs Committee, 1969. N-38

Note on censorship.  Rettig, Solomon, Ethics
    78:151-155, Jan. 1968.                       N-39

Notes of a Dirty Old Man.  Bukowski, Charles,
    Essex House, (N. Hollywood, Calif.) 1969.    N-40

Notes on moral theology.  Springer, Robert,
    Theological Studies 28:330-335, June 1967.   N-41

Notes on the motives of reproduction.  Wyatt,
    Frederick, Journal of Social Issues 23:29-56,

76

Oct. 1967. N-42

Nouwen, Henri. <u>Intimacy</u>, Fides Publishers, 1969. N-43

Number 2 moral issue today. <u>America</u> 116:452-453, Mar. 25, 1967. N-44

O'Brien, John.  Family Planning in an Exploding
  Population, Hawthorn, 1969.                          O-1
O'Brien, R. A.  Abortion, conscience and the law,
  Tablet 222:411-412, Apr. 27, 1968.                   O-2
O'Connell, William.  The silent life, Linacre
  Quarterly 35:79-89, Aug. 1968.                       O-3
O'Connor, John.  On humanity and abortion,
  Natural Law Forum 13:127-133, 1968.                  O-4
Odd Man In.  Sagarine, Edward, Quadrangle Books,
  1969.                                                O-5
O'Donnell, Francis.  The new abortion laws, Bul-
  letin of the Guild of Catholic Psychiatrists 15:
  91-93, Apr. 1968.                                    O-6
O'Donnell, Thomas.  Abortion, Linacre Quarterly
  34:364-366, Nov. 1967.                               O-7
Offer, Daniel.  Psychological World of the Teen-
  Ager, Basic Books, 1969.                             O-8
Office of Economic Opportunity.  Family Planning,
  U.S. Govt Pub. 1969, PrEx 10. 23:6130-3             O-9
O'Mahony, Patrick.  Abortion and the soul, Month
  38:45-50, July 1967.                                 O-10
On Fighting Poverty.  Moynihan, Daniel, Basic
  Books, 1969.                                         O-11
On Fighting Poverty.  Sundquist, James, Basic
  Books, 1969.                                         O-12
On "Humanae Vitae."  Zamoyta, Vincent, Pro-
  ceedings: College Theology Society 82-92, 1968.     O-13

On humanity and abortion. O'Connor, John, <u>Nat-</u>
<u>ural Law Forum</u> 13:127-133, 1968.                                    O-14

On imposing Catholic views on others. <u>America</u>
116:273-274, Feb. 25, 1967.                                              O-15

On re-doing man. Hirschhorn, Kurt, <u>Common-</u>
<u>weal</u> 86:257-261, May 17, 1968.                                       O-16

On sexual responsibility. Ramsey, Paul, <u>Catholic</u>
<u>World</u> 205:210-216, July 1967.                                        O-17

On the institutionalization of sexuality. Sprey,
Jetze, <u>Journal of Marriage and the Family</u> 31:
432-440, Aug. 1969.                                                      O-18

On <u>Understanding Poverty</u>. Moynihan, Daniel,
Basic Books, 1969.                                                       O-19

On view: on therapeutic abortion. McCleave, P.,
<u>Journal of the Iowa Medical Society</u> 59:195-197,
Mar. 1969.                                                               O-20

One hundred therapeutic abortions. Kovacs, L.,
<u>Medical Gynaecology and Sociology</u> 4:142-145,
June 1969.                                                               O-21

<u>One-Parent Family</u>. Schlesinger, Benjamin,
University of Toronto Press, 1969.                                       O-22

One small gain: Washington, D. C. decision.
<u>Nation</u> 209:589, Dec. 1, 1969.                                       O-23

O'Neil, Robert. <u>Sexuality and Moral Responsibility</u>,
Corpus, 1968.                                                            O-24

Open city for abortion. <u>Time</u> 94:65, Nov. 21,
1969.                                                                    O-25

Opposing sides mobilize. <u>St. Anthony's Mes-</u>
<u>senger</u> 73:10-11, Apr. 1967.                                         O-26

<u>Oragenitalism</u>. Legman, G., Julian Press,
1969.                                                                    O-27

Oraison, Marc. <u>The Human Mystery of Sexuality</u>,

Sheed and Ward, 1967.                                    O-28

Oral contraceptives--are they arbortifacients?
    Medical-Moral Newsletter, Vol. 3, #2, Oct.
    1966.                                                O-29

Organizations, colleges and values.  McNamara,
    Robert, Sociological Analysis 30:125-131, Fall
    1969.                                                O-30

Osofsky, Howard.  The Pregnant Teen-Ager,
    Thomas, 1968.                                        O-31

Our Bed Is Flourishing.  McCready, Robert, Sheed
    and Ward, 1969.                                      O-32

Our most explosive sex education issue.  Hoyman,
    H., Journal of School Health 39:458-469,
    Sept. 1969.                                          O-33

Our overcrowded, underfed world.  America
    120:609, May 24, 1969.                               O-34

Outcome of pregnancy when legal abortion is
    readily available.  Huldt, L., Lancet 1:467-
    468, 1968.                                           O-35

Outside the law.  Lancet 2:148-149, July 19, 1969.  O-36

Overcoming World Hunger.  American Assembly,
    1969.                                                O-37

Overpopulation.  Riga, Peter, Pastoral Life 18:41-
    46, Nov. 1969.                                       O-38

Overview: abortion campaign in 1969.  Catholic
    Almanac 1970, pp. 152-154.                           O-39

Packard, Vance.  The Sexual Wilderness, McKay,
   1968.                                          P-1

Paganelli, Vitale.  A commentary on psychiatric
   indications for the use of contraceptives, Linacre Quarterly 36:197-201, Aug. 1969.      P-2

Paganelli, Vitale.  A physician reflects on the
   bishops' pastoral, Linacre Quarterly 36:115-118,
   May 1969.                                 P-3

Pakistani sterilization campaign.  Ehrlich, D.,
   Science News 93:306, Mar. 30, 1968.       P-4

Il Papa and the pill.  Berry, Leonard, Commonweal 90:44-46, Mar. 28, 1969.             P-5

Papal Birth Control Commission.  Schema for a
   document on responsible parenthood, National
   Catholic Reporter 3:8-12, Apr. 19, 1967.    P-6

Parent or fetus?  Schwartz, Herbert, Humanist
   27:123-126, July 1967.                   P-7

Parents are entitled to some answers.  Rice, A.,
   Nation's Schools 84:18, Nov. 1969.        P-8

Parker, Graham.  Bill C-150, Criminal Law
   Quarterly 11:267-269, May 1969.          P-9

Parker, Tony.  The Hidden World of the Sex
   Offender, Bobbs, 1969.                P-10

Past Church teachings on abortion.  McCormick,
   Richard, Proceedings, American Catholic Philosophical Association 23:131-151, 1968.    P-11

Pastorals on sex education. Catholic Mind 67:1-
   10, Dec. 1969.                                             P-12
Paul VI, Pope. Humanae Vitae, various editions
   and translations published by: St. Paul Editions
   (Boston); Paulist Press (N. Y. ) and the U. S.
   Catholic Conference (Washington, D. C. )                   P-13
Pearsall, Roland. The Worm in the Bud, Mac-
   millan, 1969.                                               P-14
Peel, John. Male-oriented fertility control ex-
   periment, Practitioner 202:677-681, May, 1969.             P-15
Peel, John. Textbook of Contraceptive Practice,
   Cambridge University Press, 1969.                          P-16
Permissiveness in the dormitories. Woodring,
   Paul, Saturday Review 52:63, Dec. 20, 1969.                P-17
Perrin, Noel. Dr. Bowdler's Legacy, Athenum,
   1969.                                                       P-18
The Person in the Womb. Berrill, Norman,
   Dodd, 1968.                                                 P-19
Perspectives in Reproduction and Sexual Be-
   havior. Diamond, Milton, Indiana University
   Press, 1968.                                                P-20
Perspectives on Pornography. Hughes, Douglas,
   St. Martin's, 1970.                                         P-21
Peterson, James. Marriage and Family Counsel-
   ing, Association Press, 1968.                               P-22
Peyton, F. Women's attitudes concerning abortion,
   Obstetrics and Gynecology 34:82-88, Aug. 1969.             P-23
Phelan, Lana. Abortion Handbook, Contact, 1969.   P-24
Philosophical Anthropology. Donceel, Joseph,
   Sheed and Ward, 1967.                                       P-25
Physician and the rights of the unborn. Diamond,
   Eugene, Linacre Quarterly 34:174-181, May 1967.   P-26

A physician reflects on the bishops' pastoral.
Linacre Quarterly 36:115-118, May 1969. P-27

Pichat, see: Bourgeois-Pichat, Jean. P-28

Pilgrim's Progress I: recent developments in
family theory. Klein, John, Journal of
Marriage and the Family 31:677-687, Nov.
1969. P-29

Pilgrim's Progress II: recent trends and prospects in family research. Ruano, Betty,
Journal of Marriage and the Family 31:688-
698, Nov. 1969. P-30

The Pill. Mintz, Morton, Beacon, 1970. P-31

The pill: a second look. Hellman, Louis, FDA
Papers 3:8, Oct. 1969. P-32

The pill: abortion is irrelevant. Rock, John,
National Catholic Reporter 1:6, Aug. 11, 1965. P-33

The pill: abortion or contraception? Homiletic
and Pastoral Review 66:340-341, Jan. 1966. P-34

The pill--does it cause abortion? Ayd, Frank,
National Catholic Reporter 1:6, Aug. 4, 1965. P-35

The Pill--Facts and Fallacies. Kistner, Robert,
Delacorte, 1969. P-36

The pill goes to Washington. Business Week
2106:31-32, Jan. 10, 1970. P-37

Pills, coils and abortion. D'Antonio, William,
Commonweal 86:193-194, May 5, 1967. P-38

Pilpel, Harriet. Right of abortion, Atlantic 223:
69-71, June 1969. P-39

Pilpel, Harriet. When Should Abortion Be Legal?
N.Y., Public Affairs Committee, 1969. P-40

Plagenz, L. States legislate reform, but hospitals
are reluctant, Modern Hospital 113:82-85, July

1969. P-41

Pliny's pheromonic arbortifacients. McCully, H.,
Science 165:236-237, July 18, 1969. P-42

Plot to kill my son. Francis, Dale, Catholic
Digest 31:20-22, Apr. 1967. P-43

Pohlman, Edward. Timing of first-births,
Eugenics Quarterly 15:252-263, 1968. P-44

Policy Guide. American Civil Liberties Union,
1967. P-45

Politics of human welfare. Blatt, Burton, Journal
of Education 152:45-50, Oct. 1969. P-46

Pomeroy, Wardell. Boys and Sex, Delacorte
Press, 1968. P-47

The Pope and the Pill. Pyle, Leo, Helicon,
1969. P-48

Popenoe, Paul. Marriage: Before and After,
American Institute of Family Relations, 1969. P-49

Popenoe, Paul. Marriage Is What You Make It,
American Institute of Family Relations, 1969. P-50

Population and Family Planning. President's Committee on Population and Family Planning, U. S.
Govt. Pub. 1968. Pr36. 8 P81/81. P-51

Population, Biology and Evolution. Lewontin,
Richard, Syracuse University Press, 1969. P-52

Population Commission. Ad hoc study, United
Nations Pub. E/CN. 9/222, 1969. P-53

Population control problems. Segal, S., Bulletin
of the New York Academy of Medicine 45:455-461,
May 1969. P-54

The Population Council. Annual Report 1969,
The Population Council, 245 Park Ave., New York,
N. Y. 10017. P-55

84

Population crisis. Carter, L., *Science* 166:722-
726, Nov. 7, 1969. P-56

Population Crisis. Ng, Larry, Indiana University
Press, 1969. P-57

Population Crisis and Use of World Resources.
Mudd, Stuart, Indiana University Press, 1969. P-58

Population Dynamics. Solomon, M.E., St. Martin's, 1969. P-59

Population Ethics. Quinn, Francis, Corpus, 1968. P-60

Population, Evolution and Birth Control. Hardin,
Garrett, Freeman (2nd ed.) 1969. P-61

Population explosion and due process. Mosk,
Stanley, *Lincoln Law Review* 1:149-165, June
1966. P-62

Population, food and environment. Ehrlich, Paul,
*Texas Quarterly* 11:43-54, Summer, 1968. P-63

Population Genetics. Van Valen, Leigh, Prentice-
Hall, 1969. P-64

Population Growth and Development. Bourgeois-
Pichat, Jean, *International Conciliation* 556:1-
81, Jan. 1966. P-65

Population Newsletter. United Nations: Department
of Economic and Social Affairs, Apr. 1968. P-66

Population policy. Davis, K., *Science* 158:730-
739, 1967. P-67

Population policy. *Social Science Quarterly* Dec.
1969. P-68

Population still exploding. Draper, William, *Global
Dialogue* 1:136-139, Oct. 1968. P-69

Population Study Commission: California. *Report to
the Governor, 1967.* Berkeley, Calif. P-70

Pospishil, Victor. The damned millions, *Homiletic*
85

and Pastoral Review 69:95-104, Nov. 1968.    P-71

Pospishil, Victor. Divorce and Remarriage, Herder
and Herder, 1967.    P-72

Post-coital contraception. Szontagh, F. E. , Medical Gynaecology and Sociology 4:38-39, Feb.
1969.    P-73

Potts, Malcolm. Abortion and the soul, Month
38:45-50, July 1967.    P-74

Potts, Malcolm. Legal abortion in Eastern Europe,
Eugenics Review 59:232-250, Dec. 1969.    P-75

Potts, Malcolm. Textbook on Contraceptive Practice, Cambridge University Press, 1969.    P-76

Poverty and the Poor. Leinwand, Gerald, Washington Square Press, 1968.    P-77

Poverty: Sign of Our Times. Schwartz, Aloysius,
Alba House, 1970.    P-78

Prague Symposium of Sexology. Medical Gynaecology and Sociology 4:100-106, April 1969.    P-79

Pregnancies conceived extramaritally. Nathan,
S. , Journal of the Royal College of General
Practitioners 18:72-81, Aug. 1969.    P-80

Pregnancy in young adolescents. Waters, J. ,
Southern Medical Journal 62:655-658, June
1969.    P-81

Pregnancy prevented and terminated, Economist
231:20, June 28, 1969.    P-82

Pregnant Teen-Ager. Osofsky, Howard, Thomas,
1968.    P-83

Prejudice U. S. A. Glock, Charles, Praeger, 1969.    P-84

Premarital sex in college. America 120:126-127,
Feb. 1, 1969.    P-85

Prenatal diagnosis and selective abortion. Lancet

2:89-90, July 12, 1969.                                           P-86

President's Committee on Population and Family
  Planning. Population and Family Planning, U.S.
  Govt. Pub. 1968, Pr36. 8 P81/81.                                P-87

Pressure to change abortion laws. Carr, Aidan,
  Homiletic and Pastoral Review 67:702-704,
  May 1967.                                                       P-88

Price of childbirth. Today's Health, 40:88, Jan.
  1970.                                                           P-89

Problems of Sex Behavior. Sagarin, Edward,
  Crowell, 1968.                                                  P-90

Problems of Youth. Ramsey, Charles, Dickenson,
  1967.                                                           P-91

Procreation among the eunuchs. Sinha, A. P.,
  Eastern Anthropologist 20:168-176, May, 1967.                  P-92

Professor Grisez and natural law. Lawler, Justus,
  New Blackfriars 48:250-255, Feb. 1967.                         P-93

Professor Williams on abortion. America 120:320,
  Mar. 22, 1969.                                                 P-94

Prognosis for the development of new chemical
  birth control agents. Djerassi, Carl, Science
  166:468-473, Oct. 24, 1969.                                    P-95

Programs for seminary pastoral counseling. Quesnell, John, Catholic Charities Review 53:9-16,
  Oct. 1969.                                                     P-96

Progress in family law. Bradway, John, Annals
  of the American Academy of Political and Social
  Science 383, May 1960.                                         P-97

Proposed abortion laws: slaughter of the innocents.
  Gest, John, Linacre Quarterly 36:47-52, Feb. 1969.   P-98

Pros and cons of abortion. Ob-Gyn News 2:#22
  p. 5, Dec. 1, 1967.                                            P-99

Protecting civil liberties: the right to have an
  abortion.   Current 95:26-28,  May 1968.                    P-100
Prudes,  lewds and polysyllables.  Smylie,  James,
  Commonweal 89:671-673,  Feb. 28,  1969.                     P-101
Psychiatric illness following therapeutic abortion.
  Simon, N. ,  American Journal of Psychiatry
  124:59-65,  1967.                                           P-102
Psychiatric indications for termination of preg-
  nancy.   Anderson, E. ,  Journal of Psycho-
  somatic Research 10:127-134,  1966.                         P-103
Psychiatric indications for termination of preg-
  nancy.   Tredgold, R. ,  Lancet 2:1251-1254,
  1964.                                                       P-104
Psychiatric indications for the use of contraceptives.
  Cavanagh,  John,  Linacre Quarterly 36:92-99,
  May 1969.                                                   P-105
Psychiatric sequelae of abortion: review of the
  literature 1935-1954.  Simon, N. ,  Archives
  of General Psychiatry 15:378-385,  1966.                    P-106
Psychoanalytical study of St.  Paul's theology
  of sex.   Eickhoff,  Andrew,  Pastoral Psy-
  chology 18:35-42,  Apr.  1967.                              P-107
Psychological World of the Teen-Ager.   Offer,
  Daniel,  Basic Books,  1969.                                P-108
Psychosexual development.   Gagnon,  John,
  Trans-Action 6:12-17,  Mar.  1969.                          P-109
Psychosexual development.   Simon,  William,
  Trans-Action 6:9-12,  Mar.  1969.                           P-110
Psychosexual developments.   Money, J. ,  Journal
  of Nervous and Mental Disorders 148:111-123,
  Feb.  1969.                                                 P-111
Psychosexual response to vasectomy.   Ziegler,
88

F., Archives of General Psychiatry 21:46-54,
July 1969.                                              P-112

Psychosexuality: the Teilhardian lacunae.  Sullivan, Dan, Continuum 5:254-278, Summer 1967.   P-113

Public attitudes.  Chappel, D., Australian Law
Journal 42:120-175, Aug. 1968.                  P-114

Public health and the law.  Curran, W., American Journal of Public Health 59:1434-1435,
Aug. 1969.                                      P-115

Public policy and the abortion laws.  America
120:239-240, Mar. 1, 1969.                      P-116

Public survey on family structure and birth control.  Girard, Alain, Sociological Abstracts
17:7, #E0647, Dec. 1969.                        P-117

Puritan Jungle.  Harrus, Sara, Putnam, 1969.    P-118

Puritans in retreat.  Economist 223:682, May
13, 1967.                                       P-119

Pyle, Leo.  The Pope and the Pill, Helicon,
1969.                                           P-120

The Quality of Urban Life. Schmandt, Henry,
Sage Publications, 1969. Q-1

Quay, Eugene. Justifiable abortion, Georgetown
Law Journal 49:156-173, Winter 1960; 395-538,
Spring 1961. Q-2

Quesnell, John. Program for seminary pastoral
counseling, Catholic Charities Review 53:9-16,
Oct. 1969. Q-3

Quiet murder. Curran, Richard, Linacre Quarterly 33:344-348, Nov. 1966. Q-4

Quinn, Francis. Population Ethics, Corpus, 1968. Q-5

Quinn, John R. Birth control and the irrelevant
Church, America 119:159-162, Sept. 7, 1968. Q-6

Rabbi charged with abortion conspiracy. <u>Na-</u>
    <u>tional Catholic Reporter</u> 6:12, Jan. 21, 1970.    R-1

Rabin, A.  Some sex differences in the attitudes
    of Kibbutz adolescents, <u>Israeli Annals of</u>
    <u>Psychiatry</u> 6:62-69, Sept. 1968.    R-2

Rainwater, Lee.  Family planning in cross na-
    tional perspective, <u>Journal of Social Issues</u>
    23:1-194, Oct. 1967.    R-3

Rakstis, Ted.  Sensitivity training, <u>Today's</u>
    <u>Health</u> 48:20-25, Jan. 1970.    R-4

Ramsey, Charles.  <u>Problems of Youth</u>, Dicken-
    son, 1967.    R-5

Ramsey, Paul.  On sexual responsibility, <u>Catholic</u>
    <u>World</u> 205:210-216, July 1967.    R-6

Ramsey, Paul.  The sanctity of life, <u>Dublin Re-</u>
    <u>view</u> 241:3-23, Spring 1967.    R-7

Ransil, Bernard.  <u>Abortion,</u> Paulist Press, 1969.    R-8

Ratcliff, J.  New facts about human reproduction,
    <u>Reader's Digest</u> 89:119-122, Dec. 1966.    R-9

Rattner, Herbert.  A doctor talks about abortion,
    <u>Catholic Mind</u> 64:45-50, May 1966.    R-10

Rattner, Herbert.  Is it a person or a thing?
    <u>Report,</u> April, 1966, 20-22.    R-11

Ravenholt, R.  AID's family planning strategy,
    <u>Science</u> 163:124, Jan. 10, 1969.    R-12

Reaching a consensus on abortion.  Leo, John,

National Catholic Reporter 3:11, Feb. 8, 1967.          R-13

Reaney, William.    Creation of the Human Soul,
    Benziger Brothers, 1932.                            R-14

Rebuttal: three position papers on birth control.
    Dollen, Charles, The Priest 23:444-447, June
    1967.                                               R-15

Recent abortion reforms.    Ziff, Harvey, Journal
    of Criminal Law 60:3-10, Mar. 1969.                 R-16

Recommendations of the American Medical Asso-
    ciation concerning sex education.    Journal of
    the Louisiana Medical Society 121:262-264, Aug.
    1969.                                               R-17

Reich, Warren.    Responsible parenthood and
    overpopulation, Thomist 39:362-433, Oct. 1966.      R-18

Reiss, Ira.    The Social Context of Pre-Marital
    Sexual Permissiveness, Holt, 1969.                  R-19

Relation of the soul to the fetus.    Jewett, Paul,
    Christianity Today 13:6-9, Nov. 8, 1968.            R-20

Relaxation of Maryland's abortion law opposed by
    bishops.    Catholic Mind 66:1-3, Mar. 1968.        R-21

Religiosity and premarital sexual permissiveness.
    Heltsley, Mary, Journal of Marriage and the
    Family 31:441-445, Aug. 1969.                       R-22

Religiosity and premarital sexual permissiveness.
    Ruppek, Howard, Sociological Analysis 30:176-
    187, Fall 1969.                                     R-23

Religious liberty and abortion.    Breig, Joseph,
    Ave Maria 103:20, Apr. 23, 1966.                    R-24

Religious orthodoxy and premarital sex.    Clayton,
    Richard, Social Forces 47:469-474, June 1969.       R-25

Report on the International Conference on Abortion.
    McHugh, James, American Ecclesiastical Review

157:328-332, Nov. 1967.                                      R-26

Report on the World Social Situation.  United
    Nations Publication E. 68. IV/9,  1969.       R-27

Research and adolescent habits.  Lelys, David,
    Pastoral Life 18:18-21, Nov. 1969.          R-28

Research on human fertility.  Hill, Reuben, In-
    ternational Social Science Journal 226-228,
    1968.                                        R-29

Responsible parenthood.  National Catholic Re-
    porter 3:8-12,  Apr. 19, 1967.               R-30

Responsible parenthood and overpopulation.
    Reich, Warren, Thomist 30:362-433, Oct. 1966.  R-31

Responsibility of Dissent.  Hunt, John, Sheed
    and Ward, 1970.                              R-32

Rettig, Solomon.  Note on censorship, Ethics
    78:151-155, Jan. 1968.                       R-33

Reuben, David.  Everything You Always Wanted
    to Know about Sex, McKay. 1969.              R-34

Rhythm method of birth control.  America 120:
    663, June 7, 1969.                           R-35

Rice, A.  Parents are entitled to some answers,
    Nation's Schools 84:18, Nov. 1969.           R-36

Rice, Charles.  Government and the copulation
    explosion, Triumph 4:16-19, Mar. 1969.       R-37

Richard, E.  Abortion act in practice, British
    Medical Journal 1:778, Mar. 22, 1969.        R-38

Riegel, Robert.  Changing American attitudes
    toward prostitution, Journal of the History of
    Ideas 29:437-452, July 1968.                 R-39

Riga, Peter.  Birth control commission: conflict,
    Pastoral Life 16:281-290, May 1968.          R-40

Riga, Peter.  Overpopulation, Pastoral Life 18:

41-46, Nov. 1969.                                         R-41

Right of abortion.   Pilpel, Harriet, Atlantic 223:
69-71, June 1969.                                    R-42

Right of the foetus to be born.   Drinan, Robert,
Dublin Review 241:365-381, Winter 1967.              R-43

Right to Abortion.   Group for the Advancement of
Psychiatry 7, #75, Oct. 1969.                        R-44

Right to be born.   Knight, Jill, Tablet 221:285-
286, Mar. 18, 1967.                                  R-45

Right to dissent.   Baum, Gregory, Commonweal
88:553-554, Aug. 23, 1968.                           R-46

Right to life.   St. John-Stevas, Norman, Gonzaga
Law Review 4:1-10, Fall 1968.                        R-47

Right to life.   Shenan, Lawrence.   Current 95:
32, May 1968.                                        R-48

Rock, John.   The pill: abortion is irrelevant,
National Catholic Reporter 1:6, Aug. 11,
1965.                                                R-49

Romanowski, Richard.   Abortion: a fetal viewpoint,
Linacre Quarterly 34:276-281, Aug. 1967.             R-50

Rorvik, David.   Making men and women without men
and women, Esquire, Apr. 1969, p. 108-115.           R-51

Rosen, Harold.   Abortion in America, Beacon,
1969.                                                R-52

Rosenberg, Chaim.   Young drug addicts, Journal
of Nervous and Mental Disorders 148:65-73,
1969.                                                R-53

Rosenfeld, Albert.   Science, sex and morality,
Life 66:37-40, June 13, 1969.                        R-54

Rosenfeld, Albert.   The Second Genesis, Prentice-
Hall, 1969.                                          R-55

Ross, Ishbel.   Sons of Adam, Daughters of Eve,

Harper and Row, 1969.      R-56

Roy, Rustum. <u>Honest Sex,</u> New American Library, 1968.      R-57

Ruano, Betty. Pilgrim's Progress II: recent trends and prospects in family research, <u>Journal of Marriage and the Family</u> 31:688-698, Nov. 1969.      R-58

Rubin, Theodore. What makes a man lovable? <u>Ladies Home Journal</u> 86:68, Oct. 1969.      R-59

Rules and the ethics of sex. Hough, Joseph, <u>Christian Century</u> 86:148-151, Jan. 19, 1969.      R-60

Rupp, J. Sperm survival in victims of sexual assault, <u>Journal of Forensic Science</u> 14:177-183, Apr. 1969.      R-61

Ruppel, Howard. Religiosity and premarital sexual permissiveness, <u>Sociological Analysis</u> 30:176-187, Fall 1969.      R-62

Ryan, Mary Perkins. <u>Love and Sexuality,</u> Holt, 1967.      R-63

Sacramentum Mundi. Herder and Herder, 5 vols.
　　1968: articles on birth control, ethics, human
　　act, etc.　　　　　　　　　　　　　　　　　S-1

Sadleir, R. Ecology of Reproduction in Mam-
　　mals, Methuen, 1969.　　　　　　　　　　　S-2

Sagarin, Edward. Odd Man In, Quadrangle
　　Books, 1969.　　　　　　　　　　　　　　　S-3

Sagarin, Edward. Problems of Sex Behavior,
　　Crowell, 1968.　　　　　　　　　　　　　　S-4

St. Augustine on Nature, Sex and Marriage.
　　Hugo, John, Scepter, 1969.　　　　　　　　S-5

St. John-Stevas, Norman. Abortion, Tablet,
　　223:662-664, July 5, 1969.　　　　　　　　S-6

St. John-Stevas, Norman. Abortion and the law,
　　Dublin Review 241:274-299, Winter 1967.　　S-7

St. John-Stevas, Norman. Abortion, Catholics
　　and the law, Catholic World 206:149-152,
　　Jan. 1968.　　　　　　　　　　　　　　　　S-8

St. John-Stevas, Norman. The English experience,
　　America 117:707-709, Dec. 9, 1967.　　　　S-9

St. John-Stevas, Norman. Right to life, Gonzaga
　　Law Review 4:1-10, Fall 1968.　　　　　　S-10

St. John-Stevas, Norman. U.S. population policy
　　and programmes, Dublin Review 241:206-221,
　　Fall 1967.　　　　　　　　　　　　　　　　S-11

Saltman, John. Sex, Love and Marriage,
　　Grosset, 1968.　　　　　　　　　　　　　　S-12

Samuels, Alec. Abortion act, 1967, <u>Medicine,</u>
<u>Science and the Law</u> 9:3-10, Jan. 1969.                    S-13

Sanctity of life. Ramsey, Paul, <u>Dublin Re-</u>
<u>view</u> 241:3-23, Spring 1967.                                S-14

Sands, Michael. The therapeutic act: an answer
to the opposition, 13 <u>UCLAIR</u> 285 (1966).                 S-15

Scharper, Phillip. The sexual revolution,
<u>Critic</u> 24:6-7, July 1966.                                S-16

Schema for a document on responsible parenthood.
<u>National Catholic Reporter</u> 3:8-12, Apr. 16,
1967.                                                        S-17

Schenk, Roy. Let's think about abortion,
<u>Catholic World</u> 207:15-17, Apr. 1968.                    S-18

Schick, Tom. A matter of life and death, <u>St.</u>
<u>Anthony's Messenger</u> 77:36-37, Aug. 1969.                S-19

Schillebeeckx, Edward. <u>Marriage: Human Reality</u>
<u>and Saving Mystery,</u> Sheed and Ward, 1966.              S-20

Schiller, Patricia. Teen-agers speak out about
sex, <u>Today's Education</u> 58:23-26, Mar. 1969.           S-21

Schlesinger, Benjamin. <u>The One-Parent Family,</u>
University of Toronto Press, 1969.                           S-22

Schmandt, Henry. <u>The Quality of Urban Life,</u>
Sage Publications, 1969.                                     S-23

Schoenfeld, Eugene. <u>Dear Doctor Hip Pocrates,</u>
Grove, 1969.                                                 S-24

<u>School Continues for Pregnant Teen-agers,</u> How-
ard, Marion, U.S. Govt. Pub. 1969, FS5.220:
20115.                                                       S-25

Schrogie, John. Clinical safety of oral contraceptives, <u>FDA Papers</u> 3:5, June 1969.                S-26

Schultz, T.P. Economic model of family planning and fertility, <u>Journal of Political Economy</u>

77:153-180, Mar. 1969.                                    S-27

Schur, Edwin.   Abortion, Annals of the American
Academy of Political and Social Science 376:
136-147, Mar. 1968.                                       S-28

Schwartz, Aloysius.   Poverty: The Sign of Our
Times, Alba House, 1970.                                  S-29

Schwartz, Herman.   Parent or the fetus, Humanist
27:123-126, July 1967.                                    S-30

Schwartz, R.   Septic Abortion, Lippincott, 1968.         S-31

Science and Controversy.   Hardin, Garrett,
Freeman, 1969.                                            S-31a

Science News Yearbook 1969/1970.   Scribner,
1969.                                                     S-32

Science, sex and morality.   Rosenfeld, Albert,
Life 66:37-40, June 13, 1969.                             S-33

Seaman, Barbara.   The Doctor's Case against the
Pill, Holt, 1970.                                         S-33a

Search for an Abortionist.   Lee, Nancy, University
of Chicago Press, 1969.                                   S-34

Sebald, Hans.   Adolescence, Appleton-Century-
Crofts, 1968.                                             S-35

Second edition: Consulting the Romans.   Barr,
Stringfellow, Center Magazine 3:39-51, Jan.
1970.                                                     S-36

Second Genesis.   Rosenfeld, Albert, Prentice-
Hall, 1969.                                               S-37

Second Ten Years.   World Health Organization,
Columbia University Press, 1968.                          S-38

Secret of Culture.   Thompson, Laura, Random,
1969.                                                     S-39

Segal, S.   Population control problems, Bulletin
of the New York Academy of Medicine 45:455-

461, May 1969. S-40

Seidl, see: Sillo-Seidl, Georg. S-41

Selling-by-sex gets sizzled. National Catholic
Reporter 6:3, Jan. 14, 1970. S-42

Semmens, James. Teen-Age Pregnancy, Thomas,
1968. S-43

Senate opens pill inquiry. Steif, William, National Catholic Reporter, issues of Jan. and
Feb. 1970. S-44

Sensitivity training. Rakstis, Ted, Today's
Health 48:20-25, Jan. 1970. S-45

Septic abortion and maternal mortality. Baker,
N., Journal of the American Osteopath Association 68:807-814, 1969. S-46

Sex and confession. Champlin, Joseph, Pastoral
Life 16: articles in May, June and July issues,
1969. S-47

Sex and Gender. Stoller, Robert, Hogarth Press,
1968. S-48

Sex and Society. Wright, Helena, Allen and Unwin,
1968. S-49

Sex and the college student. Group for the
Advancement of Psychiatry 6, #60, Nov. 1965. S-50

Sex and the Family in Jewish Tradition. Gordis,
Robert, Burning Bush Press, 1967. S-51

Sex and the New Morality. Wood, Frederick,
Association Press, 1968. S-52

Sex and the Unborn Child. Limner, Roman,
Julian Press, 1969. S-53

Sex, birth control and human life. Cohen, Carl,
Ethics 79:251-262, July 1969. S-54

Sec, Church and culture. Hitchcock, James,

Catholic World 209:17-20, Apr. 1969.     S-55

Sex differentiation in aptitude maturation during
college. Lunneborg, Patricia, Journal of
Counseling Psychology 16:463-464, Sept. 1969.     S-56

Sex education and the priest. Wilson, George,
American Ecclesiastical Review 161:325-333,
Nov. 1969.     S-57

Sex education and the roles of the school and
the Church. Calderone, Mary, Annals of the
American Academy of Political and Social Science
376:53-60, Mar. 1968.     S-58

Sex education controversy. Christianity Today 14:
34, Oct. 10, 1969.     S-59

Sex education: controversy become crisis. Education Digest 35:9-11, Nov. 1969.     S-60

Sex education in the Church. Hathaway, Alden,
Pastoral Psychology 19:7-14, May 1968.     S-61

Sex Game. Bernard, Jessie, Prentice-Hall,
1968.     S-62

SIECUS in 1969. Calderone, Mary, Journal of
Marriage and the Family 31:674-676, Nov.
1969.     S-63

Sex Information and Education Council of the
United States (SIECUS). Newsletter. 491
Park Ave. So., New York, N.Y., 10016.     S-64

Sex Information and Education Council of the
United States (SIECUS). Study Guides, 1969-
1970. Address above.     S-65

Sex, Love and Marriage. Saltman, John, Grosset,
1968.     S-66

Sex, Man and Society. Ashley-Montagu, M.A.,
Putnam, 1969.     S-67

100

Sex Offenders. Gebhard, Paul, Harper, 1965.                 S-68

Sex, Psyche, Etcetera in the Films. Tyler,
    Parker, Horizon Press, 1969.                            S-69

Sex questions that bother boys. Calderone, Mary,
    Seventeen 27:80-81, July 1968.                          S-70

Sex, religion and mental health. Calderone,
    Mary, Journal of Religion and Health 6:195-203,
    July 1967.                                              S-71

Sex, Sex, Sex. Moore, Marcena, Pilgrim Press,
    1969.                                                   S-72

Sex, Society and the Individual. Broderick,
    Carlfred, Johns Hopkins Press, 1969.                    S-73

Sexton, Patricia. The Feminized Male, Random,
    1969.                                                   S-74

Sexual differentiation in socializations. Harrington,
    Charles, American Anthropologist 70:951-956,
    Oct. 1968.                                              S-75

Sexual Health and Family Planning. Calderone,
    Mary, American Public Health Association,
    1968.                                                   S-76

Sexual Maneuvers and Stratagems. Chapman,
    Andrew, Putnam 1969.                                    S-77

Sexual perversion. Nagel, Thomas, Journal
    of Philosophy 66:5-17, Jan. 16, 1969.                   S-78

Sexual practices and ethical thought. Stotts,
    John, McCormick Quarterly 20:131-145, Jan.
    1967.                                                   S-79

Sexual promiscuity in America. Ellis, Albert,
    Annals of the American Academy of Political
    and Social Science 378:58-69, July 1968.                S-80

Sexual Reproduction. Michelmore, Susan, Natural
    History Press, Doubleday, 1964.                         S-81

101

Sexual revolution. Scharper, Philip, Critic
24:6-7, July 1966.                                    S-82

Sexual Wilderness. Packard, Vance, McKay,
1968.                                                 S-83

Sexuality. Kennedy, Eugene, Critic 27:26-31,
June 1969.                                            S-84

Sexuality and knowledge in Sigmund Freud.
Engler, Barbara, Philosophy Today 13:214-
224, Fall 1969.                                       S-85

Sexuality and Moral Responsibility. O'Neil,
Robert, Corpus, 1968.                                 S-86

Sexuality and sin. Curran, Charles E., Homiletic and Pastoral Review 68:1005-1014, Sept.
1968; 69:27-34, Oct. 1968.                            S-87

Sexuality and the college student. Calderone,
Mary, Journal of the American College Health
Association 17:189-193, Feb. 1969.                    S-88

Sexuality on the island earth. Darst, David,
Ecumenist 7:81-87, Sept. 1969.                        S-89

Sexually Active Man Past Forty. Frank, Stanley,
Macmillan, 1968.                                      S-90

Shaffer, Helen. Communal living, Editorial Research Reports, #5, vol. 2, Aug. 6, 1969.            S-91

Shannon, William. The Lively Debate, Sheed
and Ward, 1969.                                       S-92

Shaw, Russell. Abortion in Public Policy,
Family Life Bureau, N.C.W.C., 1968.                   S-93

Shaw, Russell. Abortion on Trial, Pflaum,
1969.                                                 S-94

Shaw, Russell. Abortion reform, Columbia
48:20-22, Nov. 1968.                                  S-95

Shaw, Russell. Annual battle over abortion laws,

National Catholic Reporter 5:1, Mar. 19, 1969.　　S-96

Shaw, Russell.　Easier abortion laws, National
　　Catholic Reporter 5:3, July 16, 1969.　　S-97

Shaw, Russell.　How deep will the government
　　get into birth control?　Columbia 50:6, Jan.
　　1970.　　S-98

Shaw, Russell.　The Trouble with Abortion, Na-
　　tional Right to Life Committee, 1968.　　S-99

Shea, Terence.　Are religious magazines obscene?
　　Seminar 14:23-27, Dec. 1969.　　S-100

Shenan, Lawrence.　Right to life, Current 95:32,
　　May 1968.　　S-101

Shope, David.　Level of sexual experience, Journal
　　of Marriage and the Family 29:424-433, Aug.
　　1967.　　S-102

Shope, David.　Virgins make happier marriages,
　　Marriage 51:2-7, Oct. 1969.　　S-103

Should we teach about birth control in high
　　school?　Hoyman, H., Education Digest 34:
　　20-23, Feb. 1969.　　S-104

Shriver, Eunice Kennedy.　When pregnancy means
　　heartbreak, McCalls, Apr. 1968.　　S-105

The silent life.　O'Connell, William, Linacre
　　Quarterly 35:79-89, Aug. 1968.　　S-106

Sillo-Seidl, Georg.　Artificial fertilization and
　　pregnancy, Medical Gynaecology and Sociology
　　4:238-240, Sept. 1969.　　S-107

Simms, Madeline.　Abortion, Twentieth Century
　　175:#1032, 1967.　　S-108

Simon, N.　Psychiatric illness following thera-
　　peutic abortion, American Journal of Psychiatry
　　124:59-65, 1967.　　S-109

Simon, N.   Psychiatric sequelae of abortion:
     review of the literature 1935-1964, Archives of
     General Psychiatry 15:378-385, 1966.                S-110
Simon, William.   Psychosexual development,
     Trans-Action 6:9-17, Mar. 1969.                     S-111
Simpson, George.   Biology and Man, Harcourt,
     1969.                                               S-112
Sinha, A. P.   Procreation among the eunuchs,
     Eastern Anthropologist 20:168-176, May 1967.        S-113
Situation Ethics.   Fletcher, Joseph, Westminster
     Press, 1966.                                        S-114
Six Paradoxes of Sex.   Frisbie, Richard, Claretian
     Press, 1969; U. S. Catholic 34:12-18, Nov. 1968.    S-115
Sixteen Documents of Vatican II.   The Church in
     the Modern World # 27, St. Paul Editions
     (Boston) 1967, p. 539.                              S-116
Sloane, R.   The unwanted pregnancy, New England
     Journal of Medicine 280:1206-1213, May 29,
     1969.                                               S-117
Smith, B.   Biology and the Christian faith,
     Christianity Today 13:11-14, Apr. 11, 1969;
     11-14, Apr. 25, 1969.                               S-118
Smith, B.   Homosexuality in the Bible and the
     law, Christianity Today 13:7-10, July 18,
     1969.                                               S-119
Smylie, James.   Prudes, lewds and polysyllables,
     Commonweal 89:671-673, Feb. 28, 1969.               S-120
Snags of legal abortion.   Gould, Donald, New
     Statesman 75:543-544, Apr. 26, 1968.                S-121
Social aspects of family planning.   Hill, Reuben,
     World Justice 9:167-173, Dec. 1967.                 S-122
Social Context of Pre-Marital Sexual Permis-
                          104

siveness.  Reiss, Ira, Holt, 1969.                    S-123

Social role theory.  Ziegler, Frederick, Journal
   of Marriage and the Family 30:584-591, Nov.
   1968.                                              S-124

Sodomy statutes--a need for change.  South
   Dakota Law Review 13:384-387, Spring 1968.        S-125

Solomon, M. E.  Population Dynamics, St. Martin's,
   1969.                                             S-126

Some Facts and Figures about Adolescents.
   Children's Bureau H. E. W. , 1968, FS 17. 202:
   ad7.                                              S-127

Some sex differences in the attitudes of Kibbutz
   adolescents.  Rabin, A. , Israeli Annals of
   Psychiatry 6:62-69, Sept. 1968.                  S-128

Sons of Adam, daughters of Eve.  Catholic
   World 210:83-84, Nov. 1969.                      S-129

Sons of Adam, Daughters of Eve.  Ross, Ishbel,
   Harper and Row, 1969.                            S-130

Sophists will play.  Buckley, William, National
   Review 21:1182, Nov. 18, 1969.                   S-131

Spencer, Robert.  King of the abortionists,
   Newsweek 73:92, Feb. 17, 1969.                   S-132

Sperm survival in victims of sexual assault.
   Rupp, J. , Journal of Forensic Science 14:177-
   183, Apr. 1969.                                  S-133

Spock, Benjamin.  Decent and Indecent, McCalls,
   1970.                                            S-134

Sprey, Jetse.  On the institutionalization of sexuality, Journal of Marriage and the Family 31:
   432-440, Aug. 1969.                              S-135

Springer, Robert.  Notes on moral theology,
   Theological Studies 28:330-335, June 1967.       S-136

Stafford, Frank.  Student family size, <u>Journal</u>
<u>of Political Economy</u> 77:471-477, July 1969.          S-137

Stafford, J. F.  An empirical response, <u>Catholic</u>
<u>Charities Review</u> 51:10-13, Nov. 1969.          S-138

Starting point defined.  <u>Ebony</u> 25:136-137, Nov.
1969.          S-139

Statement on sex education.  McHugh, James,
<u>Bulletin of the Guild of Catholic Psychiatrists</u>
15:143-146, July 1968.          S-140

States legislate reform, but hospitals are reluctant.  Plagenz, L., <u>Modern Hospital</u> 113:
82-85, July 1969.          S-141

Steif, William.  Senate opens pill inquiry, <u>Na-</u>
<u>tional Catholic Reporter</u> 6:11, Jan. 14, 1969;
and following issues.          S-142

Steinman, Ann.  <u>Male and female</u>: <u>fact and</u>
<u>fiction</u>, Denver, Colo., Loretto Heights
College, 1969.  pamphlet.          S-143

Step toward legal abortion.  <u>U.S. News and</u>
<u>World Report</u> 67:12, Nov. 24, 1969.          S-144

Sterilization without consent.  <u>British Medical</u>
<u>Journal</u> 2:456, May 17, 1969.          S-145

Stern, Karl.  Intersexual relationships in the
modern world, <u>Listening</u> 3:233-240, Autumn
1968.          S-146

Stern, Karl.  The man and the woman, <u>Catholic</u>
<u>Digest</u> 33:90-93, Apr. 1969.          S-147

Stewart, Bruce.  Whatever turns you on, <u>Month</u>
42:335-337, Dec. 1969.          S-148

Stoller, Robert.  <u>Sex and Gender</u>, Hogarth Press,
1968.          S-149

Storm center: SIECUS.  Dollen, Charles, <u>Pastoral</u>

<u>Life</u> 19:18-21, Feb. 1970.                                    S-150

Stotts, John.   Sexual practices and ethical thought,
      <u>McCormick Quarterly</u> 20:131-145, Jan. 1967.        S-151

<u>Strangers in the House</u>.   Greeley, Andrew, Double-
      day, 1967.                                              S-152

Strategy on abortion.   Drinan, Robert, <u>America</u>
      116:177-179, Feb. 4, 1967.                              S-153

Struggle renewed.   <u>Economist</u> 223:892, May 27,
      1967.                                                   S-154

Student family size.   Stafford, Frank, <u>Journal</u>
      <u>of Political Economy</u> 77:471-477, July 1969.        S-155

Study of sex roles.   Angrist, Shirley, <u>Journal</u>
      <u>of Social Issues</u> 25:215-232, Jan. 1969.           S-156

Suitters, Beryl.   <u>History of Contraceptives,</u>
      London, International Planned Parenthood
      Federation, 1967.                                       S-157

Sullivan, Dan.   Psychosexuality: the Teilhardian
      lacunae, <u>Continuum</u> 5:254-278, Summer 1967.        S-158

Sundquist, James.   <u>On Fighting Poverty,</u> Basic
      Books, 1969.                                            S-159

Survival against odds.   Cameron, W., <u>Journal</u>
      <u>of the Kansas Medical Society</u> 70:326-327,
      July 1969.                                              S-160

<u>Survival: Study Guide through the Phenomenon</u>
      <u>of Man.</u> 1969.   G. I. A. Publications, 2115 W.
      63rd St., Chicago, Ill., 60636.                         S-161

Sweden, sex and the college student.   Ferm,
      Deane, <u>Religious Education</u> 64:53-60, Jan.
      1969.                                                   S-162

Symposium on sex and the law.   <u>University of</u>
      <u>Colorado Law Review</u> 40:178-225, Winter 1968.       S-163

<u>Synergy</u>: Woman's Liberation Movement.   San
                            107

Francisco Public Library, Dec. 1969.          S-164

Szontagh, F. E.    Post coital contraception with
    dienoestrol, <u>Medical Gynaecology and Sociology</u>
    4:36-37, Feb. 1969.          S-165

(

Taking it off. Newsweek 74:112, Oct. 13, 1969.    T-1

Taylor, Gordon. The Biological Time-Bomb,
    World, 1969.    T-2

Teen-Age Masturbation. Dort, Nicholas, Los
    Angeles, Spartan House, 1968.    T-3

Teen-Age Pregnancy. Semmens, James, Thomas
    1968.    T-4

Teen-agers speak out. Koontz, E., Today's
    Education 58:23-26, Mar. 1969.    T-5

Teen Conflicts. Bachelor, Evelyn, Diablo Press,
    1968.    T-6

Teevan, James. Changing reference groups and
    pre-marital sex, Dissertation Abstracts 29:9A
    - 3242, 1969.    T-7

TLC for miscarriages. Newsweek 73:67, Jan.
    27, 1969.    T-8

Terrible Choice. Cooke, R., Bantam, 1969.    T-9

Test-tube baby question. Gould, Donald, New
    Statesman 77:251-252, Feb. 21, 1969.    T-10

Textbook of Contraceptive Practice. Peel, John,
    Cambridge University Press, 1969.    T-11

That celibacy survey. Fichter, Joseph, America
    116:92-94, Jan. 21, 1967.    T-12

Theologian challenges Fr. Drinan. Hunt, William,
    National Catholic Reporter 4:6, Jan. 19, 1968.    T-13

Theology of Marriage. Kindregan, Charles, Bruce,
    1967.    T-14

Therapeutic abortion. Williams, E., <u>Lancet</u>,
  1:1093-1094, May 31, 1969.                                    T-15

Therapeutic abortion act: an answer to the
  opposition. Sands, Michael, 13 <u>UCLAIR</u>
  285, 1966.                                                    T-16

Therapeutic abortion act of 1967. <u>Los Angeles</u>
  <u>Bar Bulletin</u> 43: 111-115, Jan. 1968.                   T-17

Therapeutic abortion and the psychiatrist. Aarons,
  Z., <u>American Journal of Psychiatry</u> 124:745-
  747, 1967.                                                    T-18

Therapeutic abortion: blessing or murder? Visscher, Robert, <u>Christianity Today</u> 12:6-8, Sept.
  27, 1968.                                                     T-19

Therapeutic abortion, sterilization and contraception.
  Hall, R., <u>American Journal of Obstetrics and</u>
  <u>Gynecology</u> 91:581-585, 1965.                           T-20

Therapeutic abortion--the psychiatric indication.
  <u>Dickinson Law Review</u> 72:270-280, Winter 1968.         T-21

Therapeutic abortion--the U.S. law. Fahr, S.,
  <u>Journal of the Iowa Medical Society</u> 59:197-200,
  Mar. 1969.                                                    T-22

Therapeutic abortions. Thurstone, P., <u>Journal</u>
  <u>of the American Medical Association</u> 209:229
  231, July 14, 1969.                                           T-23

Thomas, F. The Church's attitude toward sex
  distorted by Augustine, <u>U.S. Catholic</u> 32:
  58, Oct. 1966.                                                T-24

Thomas sees birth control policy change.
  Thompson, David, <u>National Catholic Reporter</u>
  4:3, July 24, 1968.                                           T-25

Thompson, David. Thomas sees birth control
  policy change, <u>National Catholic Reporter</u> 4:3,

July 24, 1968.                                          T-26

Thompson, Laura.   The Secret of Culture, Ran-
    dom House, 1969.                                    T-27

Thurstone, P.   Therapeutic abortions, Journal
    of the American Medical Association 209:229-
    231, July 14, 1969.                                 T-28

Tietze, Christopher.   Abortion, Scientific American
    220:21-27, Jan. 1969.                               T-29

Tietze, Christopher.   Bibliography of Fertility Con-
    trol, National Committee on Maternal Health
    #23, 1965.                                          T-30

Time to license parents.   Barth, Alan, Los
    Angeles Times, Dec. 28, 1969, Opinion.             T-31

Time to Plan, a Time to Work.   Hoffman, Paul,
    United Nations 1969 DP/L 108.                       T-32

Timing of first-births.   Pohlman, Edward, Eugenics
    Quarterly 15:253-263, 1968.                         T-33

Tobin, William.   Ethical and moral considerations,
    Homiletic and Pastoral Review 67:1023-1031,
    Sept. 1967; 68:48-58, Oct. 1967.                   T-34

Torrents, see: Montserrat-Torrents, Jose.           T-35

Trans-sexuals: male or female?  Berg, Roland,
    Look 34:29-31, Jan. 27, 1970.                       T-36

Tredgold, R.   Psychiatric indications for termin-
    ation of pregnancy, Lancet 2:1251-1254, 1964.     T-37

Trends and Variations in Fertility in the United
    States.   Kiserm, Clyde, Harvard University
    Press, 1968.                                        T-38

Triumph of irrelevance.   Nation 208:588-589,
    May 12, 1969.                                       T-39

Trouble with Abortion.   Shaw, Russell, National
    Right to Life Committee, 1968.                      T-40

Twilight-zone dialogue. Andrews, James, <u>Ave
Maria</u> 105:4-5, Apr. 29, 1967.                    T-41
Tyler, Parker. <u>Sex, Psyche, Etcetera in the Films,</u>
Horizon Press, 1969.                                 T-42

Unborn child. Suffolk University Law Review, 2:228-230, Spring 1968.   U-1

Unborn children defined outside humanity, Joyce, R., Arizona Register 46:6-7, Jan. 2, 1970.   U-2

Uncertain future of sex. Callahan, Daniel, National Catholic Reporter 5:8, Feb. 12, 1969.   U-3

Understanding homosexuality. Gould, Robert, Seventeen 28:90-91, July 1969.   U-4

Understanding sex in the age of the pill, Clanton, G., Christian Century 86:187, Feb. 5, 1969.   U-5

U. S. Bishops. A Statement on Celibacy, National Conference of Catholic Bishops, Nov. 14, 1969. 12p.   U-6

U. S. Bishops' resolutions. Priest 25:364-368, June 1969.   U-7

U. S. population policy and programmes. St. John-Stevas, Norman, Dublin Review 241:206-221, Fall 1967.   U-8

Universal Experience of Adolescence. Kiell, Norman, Beacon, 1969.   U-9

Unmarried marrieds on campus. Karien, Arno, New York Times Magazine 28-29, Jan. 26, 1969; 16, Feb. 16; 16, Feb. 23.   U-10

Unwanted pregnancy. Lister, J., New England Journal of Medicine 280:1463-1465, June 26, 1969.   U-11

Unwanted pregnancy. Sloane, R., New England

Journal of Medicine 280:1206-1213, May 29, 1969.                                                      U-12

Up from Pedestal. Kraditor, Aileen, ed., Quadrangle, 1968.                                            U-13

Urban life and differential fertility. Micklin, Michael, Sociological Quarterly 10:480-500, Fall 1969.                          U-14

Usdin, Gene. Adolescence, Lippincott, 1969.                                                           U-15

Use of oral contraceptives. Jones, Gavin, Studies in Family Planning 24:1-13, Dec. 1967.             U-16

Van Valen, Leigh. _Population Genetics_, Prentice-
Hall, 1969.                                                    V-1

Vasectomy and after. _Lancet_ v.1, 7555, p. 1300,
Sept. 1968.                                                    V-2

Victory for liberalism. _Economist_ 222:372, Oct.
28, 1967.                                                      V-3

Virgins make happier marriages. Shope, David,
_Marriage_ 51:2-7, Oct. 1969.                                  V-4

Visscher, Robert. Therapeutic abortion: blessing
or murder? _Christianity Today_ 12:6-8, Sept.
27, 1968.                                                      V-5

A voice was heard in Rama. _St. Anthony's
Messenger_ 74:8-9, June 1967.                                  V-6

Von Gagern, Frederick. _New Views on Sex-
Marriage-Love_, Paulist Press, 1968.                           V-7

Von Hildebrand, Dietrich. _The Encyclical
Humanae Vitae_, Franciscan Herald Press, 1969.   V-8

Walker, Brooks. The New Immorality, Double-
day, 1969.                                            W-1

Wall, L. A. Abortions: ten years experience,
American Journal of Obstetrics and Gynecology
79:510-515, 1960.                                     W-2

Walters, Orville. Contraceptives and the single
person, Christianity Today 13:16-17, Dec. 8,
1968.                                                 W-3

War on sex education. Zazzaro, Joanne, American School Board Journal 157:7-11, Aug. 1969.        W-4

Wasmuth, Carl. Abortion laws, Cleveland State
Law Review 18:503-505, Sept. 1969.                    W-5

Wassmer, Thomas. Contemporary attitudes of
the Roman Catholic Church toward abortion,
Journal of Religion and Health 7:311-323, Oct.
1968.                                                 W-6

Waters, J. Pregnancy in young adolescents,
Southern Medical Journal 62:655-658, June
1969.                                                 W-7

Way of Seeing. Mead, Margaret, McCalls, 1970.         W-8

We can't walk alone. Greeley, Andrew, Sign
48:20-23, May 1969.                                   W-9

Weaver, Jerry. Latin American Development,
American Bibliographical Center, 1969.                W-10

Weijer, John. Alberta sterilization act, University
of Toronto Law Journal 19:424-429, Sept. 1969.        W-11

Weinberg, Roy.   Laws Governing Family Planning,
    Oceana, 1968.                                          W-12
Welfare mother.   Hinds, Ilene, Christian Century
    87:17-18, Jan. 7, 1970.                           W-13
Wescott, Roger.   Language, taboo and human
    uniqueness, Bucknell Review 17:28-37, Dec.
    1969.                                                W-14
West, Donald.   Homosexuality, Aldine, 1968.        W-15
Western Reserve Law School.   Symposium: abor-
    tion and the law, Western Reserve Law Re-
    view, Vol 17, #2, Dec. 1965.                      W-16
What are the rights of the unborn child?   Byrne,
    Richard, Marriage 49:16-21, Feb. 1967.        W-17
What makes a man lovable?   Rubin, Theodore,
    Ladies Home Journal 86:68-69, Oct. 1969.     W-18
Whatever turns you on.   Stewart, Bruce, Month
    42:335-337, Dec. 1969.                           W-19
Whelan, Charles.   Evolution in the law, America
    122:11-12, Jan. 10, 1970.                        W-20
When pregnancy means heartbreak.   Guttmacher,
    Alan, McCalls 95:60-61, Apr. 1968.           W-21
When pregnancy means heartbreak.   Shriver,
    Eunice Kennedy, McCalls 95:62, Apr. 1968.     W-22
When Should Abortion Be Legal?   Norwick,
    Kenneth, Public Affairs Committee, 1969,
    pamphlet.                                            W-23
When Should Abortion Be Legal?   Pilpel, Harriet,
    Public Affairs Committee, 1969.               W-24
Where is the abuse?   Economist 232:24, July 12,
    1969.                                                W-25
White, Lynn.   Machina ex Deo, MIT Press, 1969.    W-26
White, W. D.   Christian love and the loss of

intimacy, University of Portland Review 21,
# 2, 13-22, Fall 1969.                                          W-27

Who has the right to live?  Lader, Lawrence,
Good Housekeeping 166:84-85, June 1968.                         W-28

Who may not have an abortion?  Meyerowitz, S.
Journal of the American Medical Association
209:260-261, July 1969.                                         W-29

Who speaks for the fetus?  Diamond, Eugene,
Linacre Quarterly 36:58-62, Feb. 1969.                          W-30

Why birth control fails.  Lader, Lawrence, McCalls
97:5, Oct. 1969.                                                W-31

Why control birth with a knife?  Leo, John, Na-
tional Catholic Reporter 3:8, Feb. 22, 1967.                    W-32

Williams, E.  Therapeutic abortion, Lancet 1:
1093-1094, May 31, 1969.                                        W-33

Williams, George.  Professor Williams on abortion,
America 120:320, Mar. 22, 1969.                                 W-34

Williams, Harold.  The Pill in New Perspective,
Independent News Co., 1969.                                     W-34a

Wilson, George.  Sex education and the priest,
American Ecclesiastical Review 161:325-333,
Nov. 1969.                                                      W-35

Winder, Alvin.  Adolescence: Contemporary Studies,
American Book Co., 1968.                                        W-36

Wise axiom: cui bono?  America 117:292, Sept.
23, 1967.                                                       W-37

With eyes averted.  Economist 232:37, July 5,
1969.                                                           W-38

Women Around the World.  Hottel, Althea, Annals
of the American Academy of Political and Social
Science 375, Jan. 1968.                                         W-39

Women, the Law and Abortion.  Yale Reports, Yale

University Press, 1969.  W-40

Women's attitudes concerning abortion.  Peyton,
F., Obstetrics and Gynecology 34:82-88, Aug.
1969.  W-41

Wood, Frederick.  Sex and the New Morality,
Association Press, 1968.  W-42

Woodring, P.  Permissiveness in the dormitories,
Saturday Review 52:63, Dec. 20, 1969.  W-43

Worden, Thomas.  Lord, to whom shall we go?
Concilium, vol. 50, 121-138, 1969.  W-44

World Health Organization.  The Second Ten Years,
Columbia University Press, 1968.  W-45

World Population.  Farmer, Richard, Indiana
University Press, 1968.  W-46

Worm in the Bud.  Pearsall, Roland, Macmillan,
1969.  W-47

Wrage, Karl.  Children--choice or chance?  Fortress Press, 1969.  W-48

Wright, Helena, Sex and Society, Allen and Unwin, 1968.  W-49

Wright, John.  A Church of promise, Columbia
50:17-26, Jan. 1970.  W-50

Wyatt, Frederick.  Notes on the motives of reproduction, Journal of Social Issues 23:29-56,
Oct. 1967.  W-51

Wyden, Peter.  Growing Up Straight, Stein and
Day, 1968.  W-52

Yale reports. Women, the Law and Abortion, Yale University Press, 1969, 9p.  Y-1

Yearbook of the United Nations. United Nations publications, 1969.  Y-2

Year's experience. Economist 231:22, Apr. 26, 1969.  Y-3

Young drug addicts. Rosenberg, Chaim, Journal of Nervous and Mental Disease 148:65-73, 1969.  Y-4

Young male prostitute. Deisher, R., Pediatrics 43:936-951, June 1969.  Y-5

Younger, Susie. Never Ending Flower, John Day, 1969.  Y-6

Yuncker, Barbara. Baby bubble, Ladies Home Journal 86:106-107, Sept. 1969.  Y-7

Zamoyta, Vincent.   On "Humanae Vitae."   Pro-
    ceedings, College Theology Society 82-92, 1968.    Z-1
Zarrella, Mary.   College marriages, Marriage
    51:60-65,  May 1969.                                Z-2
Zawadzki, Edward.   Criminal Abortion, Thomas,
    1964.                                               Z-3
Zazzaro, Joanne.   Sex education: controversy be-
    comes crisis, Education Digest 35:9-11, Nov.
    1969.                                               Z-4
Zazzaro, Joanne.   War on sex education, Amer-
    ican School Board Journal 157:7-11, Aug. 1969.      Z-5
Zero Population Growth.   Los Altos, Calif.,
    Newsletter.                                         Z-6
Ziegler, Frederick.   Psychosexual response to
    vasectomy, Archives of General Psychiatry
    21:46-54,  July 1969.                               Z-7
Ziegler, Frederick.   Social role theory, Journal
    of Marriage and the Family 30:584-591, Nov.
    1968.                                               Z-8
Ziff, Harvey.   Recent abortion reforms, Journal
    of Criminal Law 60:3-10,  Mar. 1969.                Z-9

# ABORTION IN CONTEXT

## Subject Index

Africa, B 48, H 47, I 25.
Agency for International Development, R 12.
alternatives, B 51, S 24, V 5.
American Law Institute, Q 2.
American Medical Association, A 111, M 64, R 17, T 28.
American Public Health Association, K 12.
Anglican position, C 62.
animation, B 26, B 67, B 72, D '44, J 2, J 5, O 10, P 74,
     R 10, R 11, R 14, R 50.
anthropology, D 45, H 7, R 52, S 113.
Appalachia, D 17.
artificial insemination, D 2, F 47, R 34, R 51, S 24, S 107.
     See also: test-tube babies.
Asia, D 4, F 14, F 49, H 10, H 47, I 25, L 1, Y 6.
Association for the Study of Abortion, N 30.
Augustine, St., H 63, T 24.
Australia, C 45, H 47.
authority, B 16, C 115, C 117, F 51, H 60, H 71, H 76,
     M 7, N 34, S 92.

babies, A 114, B 57, B 63, B 77, C 47, C 121, F 47, G 3,
     G 4, H 2, L 43, M 10, M 65, N 31, P 89, R 34,
     R 51, S 107, T 2, W 48, Y 7.   See also: children,
     fetus, infants, test-tube babies, unborn child, un-
     wanted child.
beginning of life, see: animation, life.
behavioral study, F 25, M 48, S 4, S 32.
bibliography, N 25, Q 2, S 65, S 110, T 30, W 10.
biology, A 105, B 68, D 18, F 47, G 27, H 5, H 19, H 20,
     I 26, J 2, J 5, L 36, M 2, M 48, M 65, O 29,
     R 9, R 55, S 112, S 118, T 2, W 11.   See also:
     animation, life.
Birch Society, see: John Birch Society.
birth, A 129, C 100, D 20, D 47, D 55, H 2, H 3, M 65,
     P 44, P 89, R 34, S 24, S 65.
birth control, see: contraception.
birth rate, D 17, M 66, M 80, T 2.
bishops, A 84, A 85, B 51, B 52, B 54, E 16, F 31, N 26,
     P 3, P 12, R 21, U 6, U 7.
Bowdler, P 18, S 120.

California, B 69, B 70, C 9, C 46, H 72, L 16, L 17,
     M 70, N 40, P 70, T 28.
Canada, B 48, B 51, F 36, P 12, W 11.
canon law, F 51, H 78, N 32, O 15.
castration, S 113.
Catholic Church, see: Roman Catholic position.

C 6, C 8, C 14, C 16, C 24, C 37, C 54, C 55,
C 68, C 74, C 93, C 117, C 118, D 1, D 4, D 6,
D 20, D 37, D 40, D 41, E 12, E 13, F 10, F 14,
F 23, F 42, F 49, F 55, F 57, G 5, G 9, G 12,
G 14, G 17, G 21, G 46, G 48, G 49, H 1, H 5,
H 21, H 22, H 30, H 32, H 39, H 40, H 52, H 56,
H 57, H 60, H 65, H 77, L 6, L 14, M 1, M 2,
M 8, M 10, M 47, M 56, M 60, N 29, N 34, N 36,
O 1, O 9, P 2, P 6, P 15, P 16, P 49, P 51, P 76,
P 82, Q 6, R 3, R 12, R 35, R 40, S 1, S 24, S 26,
S 27, S 92, S 157, T 26, V 7, W 3, W 12, W 27,
W 48, W 49, Z 7.
contraception I. U. D., C 55, D 6, E 11, F 49, G 12, H 60,
W 34a.
contraception, oral, A 139, B 4, B 27, C 26, C 68, C 70,
D 6, D 37, D 40, D 41, F 22, F 49, G 12, G 25,
H 25, H 60, J 6, K 1, K 13, M 68a, N 29, O 29,
P 120, R 34, R 49, S 24, S 26, S 33a, S 142, Z 8.
contraception, post-coital, S 165.
controversy, A 47, A 54, A 63, A 85, A 91, A 116, B 5,
B 20, B 40, B 51, B 69, B 74, C 8, C 14, C 20,
C 24, C 117, D 29, D 40, D 41, D 44, D 54, F 36,
F 46, G 11, G 21, G 27, G 36, G 50, H 6, H 18,
H 27, H 52, H 56, H 58, H 60, H 71, H 77, K 6,
K 22, L 14, L 30, M 10, M 18, M 24, M 27, M 54,
M 60, O 15, P 40, S 15, S 33a, S 59, S 96, S 154,
W 34, Z 4.
cost, A 48, O 39, P 89.
counseling, A 110, B 32, C 72, E 9, G 3, G 4, N 43,
O 31, P 22, Q 3, U 15.
courts, A 71, A 73, C 9, C 102, F 20, F 21, H 30, N 33,
O 23.
crime, C 108, F 43, G 7, G 19, H 11, L 48, P 9, P 10,
R 1, R 61, S 125, Z 9.
culture, A 105, B 10, B 22, B 62, B 70, C 16, C 70,
C 98, C 111, C 112, D 7, D 10, D 12, D 16, E 7,
E 17, E 21, F 26, G 18, H 7, H 14, H 38, H 40,
H 62, K 2, K 5, M 21, M 57, N 40, P 1, P 10,
P 18, S 3, S 134, T 1, T 7, T 27, T 42, U 15,
W 26, W 42.
current status, A 69, A 133, B 23, B 48, C 13, C 77,
G 8, G 24, H 14, H 21, M 7, M 81, N 29, O 39,
T 26, Z 9.

D. N. A., H 4.
"day after" pill, S 165.
death, A 58, B 6, C 122, D 26, F 46, G 19, L 9, M 51

M 21, M 40, M 47, M 56, M 60, M 89, N 21, N 44, O 1, O 2, O 7, O 24, P 85, Q 5, R 8, R 33, R 41, R 54, R 55, R 63, S 1, S 16, S 134, S 136, S 151, T 34, V 5, V 7, W 42, W 49.

ethnography, B 7.

eugenics, P 44, P 75.

eunuchs, S 133.

Europe, A 69, B 48, C 105, G 22, H 22, H 47, M 20, M 30, M 63, P 75, P 79, P 82, R 38, S 6, S 9.

euthanasia, D 26, G 19.

Eve, R 56, S 129.

evolution, D 18, D 45, H 5, L 36, W 20.

extra-marital sex, N 4, R 34, S 24. See also: sex.

family, A 110, A 114, B 2, B 11, B 35, B 57, B 62, B 76, C 5, C 42, C 54, C 112, D 10, D 43, E 7, E 31, F 10, F 23, G 14, G 20, G 22, G 30, G 34, H 3, H 34, H 47, J 4, K 8, K 10, K 15, L 43, M 10, M 85, O 28, P 6, P 12, P 22, P 44, P 50, Q 3, R 18, R 27, R 58, S 22, S 23, S 30, S 91, S 137. See also: fathers, mothers, parents.

family planning, B 23, C 5, C 8, C 55, D 4, D 41, F 10, F 49, G 5, G 14, G 17, G 21, G 48, G 49, H 21, H 22, H 32, H 41, J 6, L 3, L 6, M 1, M 10, O 1, O 9, P 16, P 51, P 53, R 3, R 12, R 18, S 27, W 12, W 48. See also: contraception.

famine, H 5, N 31, O 34.

fathers, B 21, E 9, E 31, G 3, G 4, L 49a, P 6, R 18, S 24. See also: family, parents.

Federal Drug Administration, F 22, H 25, S 26.

feminine psychology, A 118, B 24, C 44, C 48, D 7, D 23, E 30, G 38, H 14, H 16, H 47, H 75, K 20, L 3, L 31, L 43, L 54, M 2, M 30, M 55, O 28, P 1, P 2, P 23, R 59, S 65, S 103, S 110, S 117, S 143, S 147, S 149, V 7, W 27. See also: women.

fertility, B 60, C 18, C 54, C 68, D 17, G 27, H 22, H 31, H 39, K 3, K 12, K 25, M 66, P 15, R 3, S 24, S 27, S 107, T 30.

fetus, A 129, B 67, B 77, C 100, C 102, D 26, D 27, D 28, D 44, D 47, D 53, H 2, I 5, J 2, J 5, J 7, K 16, L 5, L 6, L 42, M 1, N 4, O 3, O 10, P 100, R 10, R 11, R 50, S 10, S 19, S 24, S 30, S 101, S 117, T 37, U 1. See also: babies, infants, unborn child.

films, see: movies.

food, E 13, L 27, M 86, N 31, R 18.

force, F 42, O 15.

France, G 14.
Freud, Sigmund, E 22, S 163.

Gallup Poll, B 11.
gangs, B 2, C 22, L 27, R 5, S 23.
gas embolus, A 58.
generation gap, F 30, S 24. See also: hippies.
Genesis, R 55.
genetics, C 116, H 4, H 35, V 1, W 11.
genitals, H 7, L 26, M 2, M 65, P 10, P 16, R 34, S 24.
gentiles, F 19.
geriatrics, D 18, F 48, S 65.
ghetto, D 12, J 4, L 27, M 84, S 23.
goyyim, F 19.
groups, B 8, R 4, S 24, T 7, W 27.
growth, B 63, D 59, G 2, R 5, S 24, S 111.

Harvard Divinity School, H 15, H 59.
hate, F 37.
health, A 31, A 43, B 55, C 5, C 123, G 3, H 56, K 12,
    S 24, T 30, W 45. See also: mental health,
    physician, venereal disease.
Health, Education and Welfare, Dept., C 52, G 3, H 21.
Health Insurance Institute, P 89.
heredity, D 18.
hippies, A 98, C 103, R 34, R 53, S 24, S 91. See also:
    youth.
history, B 10, B 48, C 25, C 77, F 55, G 30, H 14,
    H 78, M 8, M 9, N 29, N 32, N 36, N 37, Q 2,
    R 14, S 151.
Holland, H 22.
homosexuality, A 108, B 24, C 45, C 69, C 79, C 108,
    D 16, E 24, F 36, F 43, G 28, G 39, H 16, H 40,
    M 17, M 69, N 1, N 43, R 34, R 53, S 3, S 4,
    S 24, S 65, S 74, S 113, S 119, W 15, W 52. See
    also: lesbianism, trans-sexual.
hope, K 17, S 1.
hospitals, A 69, B 7, C 33, C 126, H 21, H 24, K 19,
    L 1, L 24, P 41, P 89, T 8, T 28, W 2. See
    also: physician.
House of Lords, A 42.
human dignity, see: man.
Human Life, B 54, H 18, M 7, P 3, W 50.
"Humanae Vitae", B 54, C 118, H 18, H 71, M 7, P 13,
    Q 6, S 92, V 8, Z 1.
hunger, E 13, H 5, I 25, M 86, N 31, O 34, O 37.

illegitimacy, B 8, C 47, E 7, G 3, G 4, I 3, K 12, O 31,
    S 24, W 7.
Illinois, A 84, B 52, C 22, I 2, M 22.
India, B 48, D 4, G 5.
Indians, T 27.
infants, B 63, B 77, C 47, G 3, G 4, G 11, H 47, M 65,
    P 89, S 24, S 117.  See also: babies.
Institute for Sex Research, G 7.
intercourse, D 20, D 23, G 18, H 26, L 42, M 2, M 10,
    M 48, M 65, N 40, P 16, P 49, R 34, R 37, S 24,
    S 165.  See also: orgasm, sex.
International Conference on Abortion, C 40, M 6, M 15.
interfaith, see: ecumenism.
inter-personal relations, B 2, B 71, D 23, H 34, M 2,
    N 43, O 28, R 19, R 59, S 146, T 7, V 7, W 27.
intra-uterine device, (I.U.D.), C 55, D 6, E 11, G 12,
    H 60, N 29, W 34a.
Israel, R 2.

Japan, H 10, L 1.
Jesuit, A 116.
Jewish position, F 19, F 23, G 20, I 12, K 14, R 1, W 16.
John Birch Society, B 40, C 8.
Joseph Kennedy, Jr., Foundation, H 15, H 59.

Kansas, C 18, W 2.
Kennedy, Joseph, Jr., Foundation, H 15, H 59.
kibbutz, R 2.
killing, G 19, L 30, R 7, V 5.
Kinsey, K 10.
knowledge, E 22, F 57, H 13, R 34, S 24.  See also:
    public opinion.
Korea, Y 6.

Lambeth Resolution, D 2.
Latin America, A 127, B 48, G 17, H 47, I 25, R 3,
    W 10, W 38.
law, A 39, A 41, A 68, A 69, A 71, A 74, A 86, A 112,
    A 135, B 28, B 69, B 74, C 9, C 13, C 23, C 45,
    C 78, C 99, C 108, D 2, D 49, E 15, F 1, F 21,
    F 43, F 50, G 10, G 13, G 22, H 10, H 12, H 23,
    H 30, H 77, I 2, K 6, K 27, L 10, L 16, L 49,
    M 59, M 73, M 83, N 12, N 25, N 38, O 2, O 15,
    P 9, P 41, P 119, Q 2, R 38, S 7, S 10, S 95,
    S 119, S 144, S 163, U 1, W 5, W 12, Y 1, Z 9.
    See also: legislation.
lawyer, L 17.

legislation, A 11, A 39, A 67, A 69, A 73, A 83, A 109,
      A 113, A 136, B 62, B 69, B 73, B 75, C 10,
      C 21, C 27, C 46, C 102, C 123, D 32, D 52, E 31,
      F 20, F 39, F 45, G 8, G 26, H 11, H 15, H 33,
      I 5, J 7, K 26, L 4, L 12, L 48, M 20, M 70,
      M 80, N 20, O 6, O 23, P 40, P 116, Q 2, R 52,
      S 8, S 13, S 96, S 125, T 21, V 3, W 11, W 16,
      Z 3.   See also: law.
lesbianism, B 24, H 16, K 23, N 1, R 34, S 24.   See also:
      homosexuality.
liberty, B 64, K 11, S 145, S 164, W 44.   See also: civil
      rights.
life, A 129, B 26, B 54, B 67, B 72, C 74, D 2, D 44,
      D 47, F 47, F 56, G 19, G 27, G 50, I 5, J 2,
      J 5, J 7, K 16, L 5, L 9, L 56, M 6, O 3, O 10,
      P 39, P 74, P 100, R 7, R 10, R 11, R 14, R 50,
      R 55, S 10, S 19, S 65, S 101, S 161, U 1, W 16.
literature, D 7, D 42, H 14, H 62, K 10, K 15, K 24, P 18,
      Q 2, R 58, S 65, S 110.
litigation, A 73, C 9, F 21, H 30, N 33.
lobbying, C 27, D 54, H 33, O 39, S 108.
Lou Harris Poll, R 54.
Louisiana, A 41, G 21.
love, B 2, C 48, C 105, D 7, D 20, D 40, D 43, F 37,
      F 38, G 46, K 8, M 10, R 34, R 59, R 63, S 1,
      S 12, S 24, S 135, S 146, S 161, V 7, W 27.


magisterium, M 8.
mammals, S 2.
man, A 130, B 21, B 54, B 58, C 44, C 74, C 119, D 25,
      D 40, D 45, E 30, F 37, F 51, G 19, H 14, H 31,
      H 35, I 26, J 2, J 5, K 11, M 30, M 49, M 72,
      N 6, O 24, O 28, P 15, R 11, R 57, R 59, R 63, S 1,
      S 20, S 112, S 143, V 7, W 3, W 14, W 51.   See
      also: masculine psychology.
manuals, B 34, B 65, G 48, M 48, P 16, P 24, P 76,
      R 34, S 24.
marijuana, see: drugs.
marriage, A 110, B 32, B 62, C 48, D 23, D 40, F 31,
      F 37, G 18, G 45, H 47, H 63, K 2, K 3, K 4,
      K 8, M 10, M 47, M 58, M 72, O 28, P 22, P 49,
      P 50, P 71, P 72, P 76, Q 3, R 57, S 1, S 12,
      S 20, S 102, S 103, S 135, V 2, V 7, W 48, Z 2,
      Z 8.
Maryland, P 12, R 21.
masculine psychology, A 118, B 21, B 24, C 44, C 119,
      D 7, D 16, E 30, F 48, G 2, G 7, H 7, H 14, H 75,

I 26, L 26, L 31, M 2, M 30, O 8, O 28, P 1,
    P 10, P 15, R 34, R 59, R 62, S 24, S 65, S 74,
    S 143, S 147, S 149, T 42, V 2, W 51, Z 7. See
    also: man.
masturbation, C 119, D 46, L 26, M 48, M 56, O 8, P 47,
    R 5, R 34, S 24, S 65.
mathematics, H 65.
maturity, D 59, L 54, O 24, R 6.
medicine, A 3, A 86, A 111, A 138, B 6, B 12, B 34,
    B 40, B 63, B 66, C 18, C 21, C 26, C 46, C 68,
    C 121, C 123, C 126, D 8, D 18, D 20, D 26, E 15,
    F 1, F 40, G 12, H 1, H 2, H 15, H 16, H 25,
    H 65, H 72, I 8, J 2, J 5, K 1, K 10, K 13, K 19,
    K 25, L 1, L 9, L 11, L 24, L 43, L 49, M 3,
    M 10, M 19, M 37, M 48, M 60, M 64, M 68, M 89,
    N 4, O 29, P 16, P 41, P 75, P 76, P 82, P 86,
    P 89, P 99, Q 2, R 10, R 11, R 38, R 52, R 61,
    S 24, S 33a, S 117, T 8, T 28, W 2, W 11, W 45.
    See also: physician, venereal disease.
mental health, A 31, A 43, C 5, M 69, R 4, R 53, S 109,
    S 110, S 138, S 139, T 21, T 37.
Michigan, A 83, C 72.
middle America, S 74.
Midnight Cowboy, S 148.
minorities, A 108, B 35, D 12, E 24, F 43, G 15, H 8,
    L 27, S 3, T 27. See also: civil rights, Negro,
    race.
Model Penal Code, Q 2.
moral theology, A 116, B 9, B 32, B 76, C 13, C 24,
    C 30, C 62, C 111, C 115, C 117, C 119, C 120,
    D 2, D 49, D 52, F 40, G 19, H 13, K 4, K 8,
    K 22, L 32, M 4, M 5, M 7, M 8, O 10, O 24,
    P 71, P 72, S 136, T 34. See also: ethics, "new
    morality," situation ethics.
mortality, A 58, B 6, D 26, F 46, G 19, M 51.
mothers, A 58, A 114, B 6, B 63, C 100, C 122, D 26,
    D 47, F 57, G 4, G 38, H 34, K 10, L 3, M 51,
    P 6, R 18, R 56, S 10, S 22, S 24, S 30, S 101,
    S 109, T 30, T 37, W 7. See also: family, parents
    rights, women.
movies, E 21, H 14, S 65, S 148, T 42.
murder, C 122, F 46, G 11, G 19, V 5.
mutilation, H 7, R 34.

narcotics, C 103. See also: drugs
National Commission on Human Life and Reproduction, N 6.
National Committee on Maternal Health, T 30.

National Council on Illegitimacy, E 9.
National Right to Life Committee, N 7.
natural law, C 99, C 116, D 2, G 36, H 23, H 63, L 14,
    M 13, N 32, N 36, O 4.
Negro, B 35, D 12, H 8, L 31, S 139.  See also: civil
    rights, minorities, race.
New Jersey, A 85, P 12.
"new morality, " B 9,  F 38,  G 9,  S 24,  S 52,  W 42.  See
    also: situation ethics.
New Orleans, A 69.
New York, A 67, A 68, B 20, C 23, M 59, N 25, N 26,
    N 27, N 28, N 29, T 39.
newsletters, A 110, A 133, M 60, N 6, N 7, N 30, P 66,
    S 64, Z 6.
Nixon, President, F 42, P 51, P 87.
North Carolina, N 20.
nudity, B 22, E 21, M 48, N 40, R 34, S 24, T 1.

obscenity, S 100, S 134.  See also: pornography.
Office of Economic Opportunity, S 159.
Ohio, A 113.
opposition, A 47, A 63, A 80, A 85, A 91, A 135, A 136,
    A 137, B 5, B 20, B 51, B 52, B 69, B 75, B 76,
    C 8, C 14, C 20, C 23, D 29, D 43, D 54, F 36,
    F 46, F 50, G 11, G 36, G 50, H 18, H 27, H 52,
    H 58, H 60, H 71, H 77, I 2, K 6, L 11, L 30,
    L 55, M 18, M 24, M 27, M 54, M 60, N 6, N 7,
    N 28, O 15, O 26, P 116, Q 2, R 37, R 49, S 10,
    S 15, S 33a, S 99, V 6.
orgasm, M 2, M 10, M 48, M 65, N 40, P 49, R 34,
    S 24.  See also: intercourse.
osteopaths, B 6.
over-population, See: population.
ovulation, C 68, M 48, M 65, P 49, R 34, S 24.

Pakistan, E 12.
Papal Birth Control Commission, D 41, H 60, P 6, R 40.
parents, B 11, B 21, D 43, E 7, E 31, G 3, G 4, G 30,
    G 49, H 34, L 49a, P 6, R 18, R 36, S 22, S 30,
    W 52.  See also: family.
Paul, St. , E 14, F 31.
Paul VI, pope, B 27, B 54, C 30, C 63, D 41, H 18,
    H 60, H 71, P 6, P 13, P 120, Q 6, R 40, S 92,
    V 8, W 50, Z 1.
permissiveness, H 26, K 11, P 85, R 19, R 39, R 62,
    S 148, T 7, W 43.
person, see: man.

Philippines, J 4.

philosophy, C 99, D 8, D 40, D 45, D 49, E 22, F 38,
G 9, G 19, G 36, H 23, J 2, J 5, M 9, M 21, N 1,
S 1, W 1.

physician, A 105, A 109, B 7, B 34, C 33, C 68, C 122,
C 126, D 8, D 27, E 15, H 24, H 72, K 19, L 1,
L 9, L 11, L 18, M 10, M 19, M 37, M 64, M 68,
P 3, P 41, P 82, P 86, R 10, R 49, S 24, S 33a,
S 132, T 8, U 15, V 7, W 2.   See also: hospital,
medicine.

physiology, M 2, M 48, M 65, O 29, R 34.   See also:
biology.

"the pill", see: contraception, oral.

Planned Parenthood Association, C 1, D 6, D 43, S 157.

Playboy philosophy, W 1.

Pliny, M 11.

pluralism, A 32, A 54, F 50, I 12, O 15.   See also:
ecumenism.

politics, B 58, H 8, H 33, I 25, M 84, R 56, S 11, S 93,
S 98.

population, A 117, B 57, B 60, C 28, D 9, D 48, E 13,
F 10, F 14, F 17, F 42, G 12, G 14, H 5, H 31,
H 39, I 25, K 10, L 30, L 36, M 58, M 80, M 86,
N 29, N 31, O 1, O 34, O 37, P 51, P 53, P 55,
P 66, P 68, P 70, P 87, Q 5, R 18, R 41, S 11,
S 40, S 126, T 2, V 1, W 10, Z 6.

pornography, H 62, K 24, R 34, S 24.   See also: obscenity.

poverty, B 58, C 54, D 17, H 5, H 8, H 34, I 25, L 27,
M 62, M 84, M 85, N 31, O 34, O 37, S 23, S 29,
S 159, Y 6.

Prague, Czechoslovakia, P 79.

pregnancy, A 115, C 72, D 47, D 53, F 57, G 3, G 4,
G 21, G 50, H 2, H 3, H 47, H 55, H 65, I 8,
K 12, K 25, L 1, L 3, L 6, L 43, M 1, N 4, O 3,
O 31, P 82, P 86, R 11, R 34, S 24, S 30, S 43,
S 105, S 107, T 37, U 1, W 7.   See also: mothers.

prejudice, G 15.

pre-marital sex, C 48, C 71, F 57, H 26, N 4, P 85,
R 19, R 34, R 39, R 62, S 24, S 65, T 7.   See
also: promiscuity, sex.

prenatal, see: pregnancy.

progestin, C 68.

promiscuity, E 17, F 57, M 48, R 34, S 24.   See also:
sex.

promise-keeping, G 34.

prostitution, D 16, D 58, E 17, N 40, R 34, R 39, S 24,
Y 6.

Protestant position, A 55, B 9, B 20, B 72, C 17, C 40,
        C 62, C 70, C 93, C 111, D 7, D 51, E 14, F 36,
        F 50, G 23, G 34, G 45, H 17, H 48, H 66, I 12,
        J 2, L 19, M 73, M 87, O 15, R 52, R 60, S 52,
        S 118, S 119, S 151, V 5, W 3, W 48. See also:
        religion, Roman Catholic position.
psychiatry, A 1, A 43, A 115, A 136, B 24, B 71, C 37,
        E 22, G 38, G 39, H 16, H 24, K 23, K 26, L 32,
        M 16, O 6, P 2, S 109, S 110, T 21, T 31, Z 7.
        See also: mental health, physician.
psychology, A 43, A 105, A 118, B 25, B 32, B 71, C 5,
        C 105, D 30, E 14, E 30, G 2, G 5, G 28, H 14,
        H 17, H 40, K 24, M 2, M 17, N 1, N 43, O 8,
        O 24, O 28, P 22, R 2, R 3, S 111, S 134, T 42,
        V 7, W 36. See also: psychiatry.
psychosexuality, G 2, M 69, S 111, S 158, Z 7.
puberty, C 4, C 119, D 46, M 69, O 8, R 5, R 34, S 1,
        S 24, U 15. See also: adolescence, teen-ager.
public health, A 69, A 86, B 55, C 6, C 45, C 123, G 3,
        G 21, H 3, H 21, K 12, P 70, R 53, W 45.
public opinion, A 28, A 47, B 40, B 68, C 45, F 36, F 57,
        G 14, H 27, H 58, L 29, P 23, P 116, R 39, S 18,
        S 95, V 6, W 6. See also: knowledge.
puritan heritage, D 7, D 58, H 14, H 38, P 14, P 18,
        P 119, R 34, S 120.

Quinn, John, bishop, M 7, Q 6.

race, B 35, D 12, G 15, H 8, L 27, M 62, S 3, T 27.
        See also: Minorities, Negro.
rape, C 62, G 7, P 10, R 34, R 61, S 24.
Reagan, Governor, P 70.
Recovery, Inc., S 3.
reform, A 29, A 67, A 68, A 83, A 112, A 113, B 62,
        B 75, B 76, C 14, C 23, C 27, C 45, C 108, D 32,
        E 15, F 36, F 50, G 11, G 13, H 12, I 2, L 4,
        L 10, L 16, M 27, N 12, N 27, O 6, P 9, P 41,
        S 97, T 39, V 3, Z 9.
religion, A 74, B 64, B 72, C 3, C 5, C 14, C 17, C 39,
        C 70, C 71, C 72, C 118, D 25, E 14, F 50, F 51,
        G 15, G 45, H 17, H 26, H 38, H 66, I 12, J 2,
        K 17, K 22, L 28, L 44, L 48, M 9, M 21, M 60,
        M 62, M 72, N 34, N 37, O 2, P 12, P 18, P 71,
        P 74, Q 3, Q 6, R 8, R 52, R 62, S 20, S 100,
        S 118, S 119, S 120, W 42. See also: natural law.
reproduction, B 68, C 68, D 30, F 47, G 27, H 20, M 10,
        M 48, M 65, N 6, R 9, R 54, S 2, S 24, S 113,

136

W 51.   See also: intercourse.
Reproductive Biology Research Foundation,  B 68.
research,  A 133,  B 57,  C 52,  C 54,  C 68,  C 112,  C 116,
        D 30,  D 37,  D 41,  F 32,  F 47,  G 7,  G 12,  G 27,
        H 4,  H 7,  H 22,  H 25,  H 30,  H 66a,  J 2,  J 5,
        K 15,  L 28,  M 1,  M 48,  M 60,  M 68a,  O 8,  P 15,
        R 3,  R 11,  R 58,  S 32,  S 33a,  S 157,  S 165,  T 30,
        V 1,  W 51.   See also: science.
rhythm,  D 43,  G 17,  M 10,  N 32,  R 34,  R 35.
rights,  B 64,  B 77,  C 13,  C 33,  C 69,  C 102,  D 27,  D 50,
        D 53,  E 24,  F 42,  F 43,  F 56,  G 38,  H 3,  H 40,
        I 5,  J 5,  K 16,  L 5,  P 39,  P 100,  S 10,  S 101,
        S 164.   See also: mothers, unborn child.
Rochester, N.Y. ,  M 22.
Rockefeller, Governor,  N 27.
Roman Catholic position,  A 11,  A 54,  A 67,  A 74,  A 112,
        A 116,  A 135,  A 137,  B 15,  B 52,  B 54,  B 67,
        C 14,  C 20,  C 25,  C 30,  C 63,  C 100,  C 115,
        C 117,  C 118,  D 1,  D 7,  D 41,  D 44,  D 49,  G 30,
        G 35,  H 12,  H 60,  H 71,  K 17,  L 14,  L 32,  L 44,
        L 56,  M 7,  M 8,  M 72,  N 6,  N 32,  N 35,  N 37,
        O 15,  O 28,  Q 6,  S 8,  S 94,  T 24,  U 7,  W 6,
        W 50.   See also: Protestant position, religion.
Roman Empire,  B 10.
Russia,  G 22,  P 75.


San Mateo, Calif. ,  T 28.
schools,  B 55,  C 3,  D 42,  H 55,  H 56,  H 57,  I 12,  P 12,
        S 59,  S 74,  Z 4,  Z 5.   See also: education.
science,  C 28,  C 68,  D 8,  D 37,  F 47,  G 27,  H 4,  H 6,
        H 20,  H 25,  H 30,  H 39,  I 26,  J 2,  J 5,  K 1,
        K 13,  L 35,  M 48,  M 68,  O 29,  R 11,  R 54,  R 61,
        S 13,  S 32,  S 65,  T 29,  V 1.   See also: research.
Senate, U.S. ,  S 142.
sensitivity,  B 71,  R 4.
sex,  A 130,  B 4,  B 22,  B 25,  B 65,  B 68,  B 70,  C 4,
        C 6,  C 15,  C 22,  C 39,  C 70,  C 71,  C 74,  C 105,
        C 120,  D 7,  D 16,  D 20,  D 23,  D 41,  D 46,  D 55,
        E 14,  E 17,  E 21,  F 26,  F 44,  F 48,  F 53,  G 7,
        G 18,  G 20,  G 27,  G 33,  G 39,  H 7,  H 14,  H 16,
        H 20,  H 26,  H 47,  H 63,  H 66,  H 69,  I 26,  K 5,
        K 10,  K 18,  L 26,  L 31,  L 42,  L 54,  M 2,  M 10,
        M 17,  M 21,  M 47,  M 48,  M 56,  M 57,  M 58,
        M 65,  M 69,  M 74,  N 4,  N 40,  P 16,  P 18,  P 47,
        P 49,  P 50,  P 79,  P 85,  R 2,  R 34,  R 37,  R 39,
        R 54,  R 57,  R 61,  S 1,  S 4,  S 12,  S 16,  S 21,
        S 24,  S 42,  S 52,  S 120,  S 125,  S 163,  S 165,  T 7,

T 42, U 15, V 7, W 42, Z 7.  See also: pre-
marital sex, sexuality.
sex education, B 2, B 5, B 40, B 55, C 2, C 3, C 4,
D 42, H 13, H 17, H 56, H 57, I 12, M 16, M 22,
P 12, R 17, R 36, S 59, S 65, W 35, W 52, Z 4,
Z 5.
Sex Information and Education Council of the United States
(SIECUS), B 65, C 8, D 42, S 64, S 65.
Sexology magazine, M 2.
sexuality, A 118, B 25, B 70, C 5, C 7, C 16, C 17,
C 44, C 48, C 71, C 98, C 112, C 116, C 120, D 7,
D 30, D 41, E 14, E 22, F 19, F 51, G 18, G 35,
G 45, G 46, H 14, H 26, H 38, H 48, H 60, H 75,
K 3, K 11, L 26, L 31, M 2, M 21, M 22, M 30,
M 56, N 1, N 5, N 43, O 8, O 24, O 28, P 1,
P 10, R 6, R 19, R 33, R 40, R 59, R 60, R 62,
R 63, S 4, S 16, S 74, S 102, S 111, S 135, S 146,
S 148, S 151, S'158, T 24, U 6, W 36, W 49.  See
also: sex.
sin, C 119, C 120, L 48, R 60.
situation ethics, B 9, F 38, G 9, S 52.  See also: ethics.
society, A 130, A 138, B 65, C 17, C 70, C 111, E 7,
E 17, F 53, G 4, H 7, H 14, H 38, H 40, H 62,
I 3, K 2, L 27, M 51, M 81, N 40, P 1, P 10,
R 19, S 3, S 16, S 23, S 29, S 74, S 135, S 146,
T 7, T 42, W 42.  See also: family, religion.
sociology, B 8, B 13, B 21, C 3, C 42, C 47, C 55,
C 71, C 112, D 30, E 7, E 9, E 17, F 31, F 32,
F 49, F 55, G 3, G 4, G 7, G 12, G 14, G 15,
G 32, H 7, H 14, H 15, H 30, H 32, H 40, H 49,
I 3, J 4, K 2, K 10, K 19, L 27, L 44, M 17,
M 25, M 66, M 85, N 31, O 24, O 31, P 22, P 68,
R 3, R 5, R 19, R 27, R 62, S 4, S 22, S 107, V 7,
Z 8.
sodomy, G 18, N 1, P 10, R 34, S 24, S 125.
soul, D 44, J 2, J 5, O 10, P 74, R 10, R 11, R 14.
Soviet, see: Russia.
sperm, R 34, R 61, S 24, V 2.
sperm, frozen, F 47, S 107.
state's rights, F 20.
statistics, A 80, C 52, D 21, S 32, Y 2.
sterility, C 18, C 54, G 12, G 46, K 3, V 2.
sterilization, D 2, D 41, E 12, H 1, H 60, R 34, S 145,
V 2.
students, see: college, schools, education.
superstition, H 13, S 24, W 14.
surveys, B 23, F 32, G 14, H 14, H 21, H 47, H 64, L 2,
R 54,

Sweden, B 48, B 55, F 26, M 20, M 81.
symposium, C 82, D 8, D 25, H 15, L 36, P 79, S 163,
    W 16.
Synanon, S 3.

taboo, W 14.
Taiwan, C 55, F 49.
teen-agers, B 2, C 4, C 52, D 46, G 32, H 55, K 7a,
    K 18, K 23, L 28, M 55, O 8, O 31, P 47, S 21,
    S 24, S 35, S 43, T 7, U 15.  See also: adolescence,
    children, hippies, puberty.
Teilhard de Chardin, S 158, S 161.
test-tube babies, A 114, F 47, G 27, R 34, R 51.  See
    also: babies.
textbook, B 34, B 65, P 16, P 24, P 76.
theatre, B 22, E 21, H 14, T 1.
trans-sexual, B 24, S 163.  See also: homosexuality.

unborn child, B 26, B 77, C 102, D 27, D 28, D 44, D 53,
    I 5, J 2, J 5, J 7, K 16, L 5, L 42, M 59, N 32,
    O 3, O 10, P 100, R 50, S 30, U 1.  See also:
    fetus, babies, rights.
underground press, B 30.
United Nations, B 60, D 21, F 10, F 14, H 41, P 53,
    P 66, R 27, W 45, Y 2.
United States, A 63, B 22, B 48, B 54, B 55, C 1, C 28,
    C 98, C 105, C 108, D 12, D 49, E 17, F 19, F 20,
    F 26, F 42, G 4, G 8, G 15, G 18, H 8, H 21,
    H 34, H 52, K 12, K 20, L 1, L 27, L 44, M 20,
    M 84, O 1, O 9, O 39, P 1, P 12, P 41, P 51,
    P 87, R 12, R 37, R 52, S 11, S 93, S 98, S 142,
    S 159, W 2, Z 9.
United States Government publications, C 52, F 22, H 21,
    H 25, H 55, O 9, P 51, P 87, S 26.
unwanted child, G 38, H 65, L 1, L 43, S 117.  See also:
    babies.
unwed mothers, B 8, C 47, E 7, F 57, G 3, G 4, H 55
    I 3, K 2, S 24.  See also: mothers, pregnancy.
urban crisis, see: cities.
usury, N 34.

values, B 54, C 2, C 13, C 14, C 48, D 7, D 30, D 40,
    E 30, F 57, I 3, K 17, M 25, M 55, S 16, W 51.
    See also: ethics.
vasectomy, A 104, E 12, H 1, R 34, S 24, V 2, Z 7.
Vatican II, Council, C 30, C 63.
venereal disease, C 22, R 34, S 24.

# ABORTION IN CONTEXT

## Sources

Alba House, S 29.
Aldine, W 15.
Allen and Unwin, W 49.
America, A 29, A 31, A 43, A 48, A 54, A 63, A 71,
     A 79, A 80, A 91, A 107, A 135, B 28, D 29,
     D 50, D 51, D 54, F 32, K 4, M 4, M 5, M 6,
     M 22, N 44, O 15, O 34, P 85, P 116, Q 6, R 35,
     S 9, W 20, W 34, W 37.
American Anthropologist, H 7.
American Assembly, O 37.
American Bibliographical Center, W 10.
American Book Co., W 36.
American Catholic Philosophical Association, Proceedings,
     D 49, M 9.
American Civil Liberties Union, A 109.
American Druggist, F 22.
American Ecclesiastical Review, A 36, A 136, G 35, M 15,
     W 35.
American Institute of Family Living, A 110.
American Institute of Family Relations, P 49, P 50.
American Journal of Nursing, G 48.
American Journal of Obstetrics and Gynecology, H 1, H 65,
     W 2.
American Journal of Psychiatry, A 1, H 24, K 23, S 109.
American Journal of Public Health, A 69, C 123.
American Medical Association, Journal, A 111, M 64, R 17,
     T 28.
American Public Health Association, see: Public Health
     Reports.
American School Board Journal, Z 5.
Annals of the American Academy of Political and Social
     Science, B 62, E 17, H 47, S 28, W 39.
Annual Review of Pharmacology, K 1.
Appleton-Century-Crofts, S 35.
Archives of General Psychiatry, S 110, Z 7.
Arizona Register, J 7.
Asia Publishing House, D 4.
Association for the Study of Abortion, A 133, N 30.
Association Press, C 22, D 59, P 22, W 42.

Atheneum,  P 18.
Atherton,  A 105.
Atlantic,  H 8,  P 39.
Australian Law Review,  C 45.
Ave Maria,  A 4,  A 117,  B 64.

Bantam,  C 100.
Basic Books,  B 23,  F 30,  H 40,  M 84,  M 85,  O 8,  S 159.
Beacon,  F 52,  H 66a,  K 7a,  M 56,  M 68,  M 68a,  R 52.
Benziger Brothers,  R 14.
Bobbs-Merrill,  L 1,  P 10.
British Medical Journal,  I 8,  R 38,  S 145.
Bruce,  K 8,  M 72.
Bucknell Review,  W 14.
Bulletin of the Guild of Catholic Psychiatrists,  M 16,  O 6.
Bulletin of the New York Academy of Medicine,  S 40.
Burning Bush Press,  G 20.
Business Week,  P 37.

California Medicine,  H 28.
California State,  P 70.
California Western Law Review,  F 43,  G 18.
Cambridge University Press,  P 16,  P 76.
Cassell,  D 58.
Catholic Almanac,  O 39.
Catholic Charities Review,  M 40,  Q 3,  S 138.
Catholic Digest,  F 46,  S 147.
Catholic Lawyer,  A 67,  A 73,  A 74,  B 74,  B 75,  C 23,
        D 52,  G 10,  N 33.
Catholic Mind,  A 84,  A 85,  B 52,  C 20,  G 17,  H 23,  L 9,
        N 26,  P 12,  R 10,  R 21.
Catholic School Journal,  M 23.
Catholic Theological Society of America,  Proceedings C 119.
The Catholic University of America,  H 78.
Catholic World,  H 38,  L 49a,  M 30,  R 6,  S 8,  S 18,  S 129.
Center Magazine,  B 10,  M 88.
Christian Century,  C 17,  C 70,  E 24,  F 36,  H 34,  H 48,
        R 60.
Christianity in Crisis,  B 20,  G 34.
Christianity Today,  C 40,  C 93,  F 50,  J 2,  L 19,  S 118,
        S 119,  V 5,  W 3.
Church Information Office (Westminister) C 62.
Churchman,  C 111.
Claretian Press,  F 53.
Clergy Review,  F 39.
Cleveland State Law Review,  W 5.
College Theology Society,  Z 1.

Columbia, H 52, S 95, W 50.
Columbia University Press, W 45.
Commonweal, A 28, A 32, B 16, B 27, B 73, C 82, D 6,
    F 31, H 19, H 35, K 28, S 120.
Concilium (Newman Press), W 44.
Concordia, H 66.
Contact, P 24.
Continuum, D 44, K 22, S 158.
Corpus, C 115, O 24, Q 5.
Criminal Law Quarterly, P 9.
Critic, F 47, K 5, S 16.
Crowell, S 4.
Current, F 45, P 100, S 101.
Current Abstracts of the Soviet Press, K 10.

Dartmouth University Press, D 8.
Day, John, Y 6.
Delacorte, B 63, K 13, L 31, P 47.
Delaware Medical Journal, M 83.
Diablo Press, B 2, G 47.
Dickenson, R 5.
Dickinson Law Review, T 21.
Dissertation Abstracts, T 7.
Dodd, B 26.
Doubleday, C 103, D 18, G 30, G 32, M 57, M 65, W 1.
Dublin Review, D 53, G 44, K 14, N 35, R 7, S 7, S 11.

Eastern Anthropologist, S 113.
Ebony, S 139.
Economist, A 47, F 34, P 82, P 119, S 154, V 3, W 25,
    W 38, Y 3.
Ecumenist, B 15, D 7, F 44, G 45, M 54.
Editorial Research Reports, S 91.
Education Digest, H 57, Z 4.
Esquire, R 51.
Essex House (No. Hollywood, Cal.), B 70.
Ethics, C 74, R 33.
Eugenics Quarterly, P 44, P 75.
Extension, L 56.

Family Digest, B 76, H 11.
Fertility-Sterility, K 3.
Fides, C 116, D 40, N 43.
Film Quarterly, E 21.
Focus on Hope, K 17.
Fordham University Press, B 32.
Fortress Press, W 48.

D 10, F 57, H 3, H 22, H 26, K 15, M 1, R 58,
    S 102, S 135, Z 8.
Journal of Nervous and Mental Disorders, M 69, R 53.
Journal of Obstetrics and Gynecology, H 3.
Journal of Philosophy, N 1.
Journal of Political Economy, S 27, S 137, S 155.
Journal of Psychosomatic Research, A 115.
Journal of Religion, B 72.
Journal of Religion and Health, C 5, C 126, W 6.
Journal of School Health, B 55, H 56.
Journal of Social Issues, A 118, R 3, W 51.
Journal of the American College Health Association, C 7.
Journal of the American Osteopath Association, B 6.
Journal of the History of Ideas, R 39.
Journal of the Iowa Medical Society, F 1, M 3.
Journal of the Kansas Medical Society, C 18.
Journal of the Louisiana Medical Society, R 17.
Journal of the Royal College of General Practitioners, N 4.
Jubilee, H 27a.
Julian Press, L 26, L 42.


Kentucky Law Journal, C 108.
Knopf, E 7.
Kummer, K 26.


Ladies Home Journal, R 59, Y 7.
Lancet, A 3, B 12, H 64, O 36, P 86, T 37, V 2, W 33.
Life, D 47, R 54.
Liguorian, K 21.
Linacre Quarterly, C 37, C 121, C 122, D 1, D 27, D 28,
    G 11, H 9, H 10, H 16, L 10, L 55, M 37, M 89,
    O 3, O 7, P 2, P 3, R 50.
Lincoln Law Review, M 80.
Lippincott, S 31, U 15.
Listening, G 9, S 146.
Little, Adam, H 49.
London Times, B 4.
Look, B 24, C 2, L 2.
Loretto Heights College, S 143.
Los Angeles Bar Bulletin, L 17.
Los Angeles Times, B 11.


McCalls, G 50, L 6, M 58, S 105, S 134, W 31.
McCormick Quarterly, S 151.
McGraw-Hill, C 3, D 20.
McKay, P 1, R 34.
Macmillan, C 14, F 48, G 46, P 14.

Marriage, A 137, B 77, C 99, K 11, S 103, Z 2.
Massachusetts Institute of Technology Press, W 26.
Medical Economics, C 21.
Medical Gynaecology and Sociology, A 128, G 12, K 19,
        P 73, P 79, S 107, S 165.
Medical Moral Newsletter, A 45, M 60, O 29.
Medical Opinion and Review, H 4.
Medicine, Science and the Law, S 13.
Mercy Hospital (San Diego, Cal.), D 43.
Methuen, S 2.
Michigan Medicine, B 40.
Millbank Memorial Fund Quarterly, C 55.
Minnesota Law Review, K 27.
Modern Churchman, G 23.
Modern Hospital, P 41.
The Month, O 10, P 74, S 148.


Nation, H 73, O 23, T 39.
National Catholic Education Association Bulletin, A 138.
National Catholic Reporter, A 68, A 116, A 139, B 51,
        C 15, C 76, E 11, E 15, H 30, H 58, H 59, H 60,
        H 77, L 29, L 30, N 5, P 6, R 1, R 49, S 42,
        S 96, S 97, S 142, T 26.
National Catholic Welfare Conference, S 93.
National Commission on Human Life and Reproduction, N 6.
National Committee on Maternal Health, T 30.
National Conference of Catholic Bishops, U 6.
National Council on Illegitimacy, E 9.
National Review, S 131.
National Right to Life Committee, N 7, S 99.
Nation's Schools, R 36.
Natural Law Forum, N 32, O 4.
New American Library, A 129, R 57.
New Blackfriars, L 14.
New England Journal of Medicine, B 66, D 26, D 32, L 43,
        S 117.
New Republic, A 57, B 22.
New Society, I 3.
New Statesman, A 42, A 97, G 24, G 25, G 26, G 27,
        H 13, M 18, M 19, M 41.
New York Bar Association Record, N 25.
New York Law Forum, M 59.
New York State, N 27.
New York Times Index, N 29.
New York Times Magazine, B 68, K 2, M 70.
New York University Press, F 23.
New Yorker, N 28.
Newsweek, A 39, A 93, S 132, T 1, T 8.

North Carolina Law Review, F 20, N 20.
North Carolina Medical Journal, B 34.
Notre Dame Law Review, A 11.

Ob-Gyn News, P 99.
Obstetrics and Gynecology, M 32, P 23.
Oceana, W 12.
Ohio Medical Journal, M 51.
Our Sunday Visitor, B 5.
Oxford University Press, B 9.

Parents Magazine, G 49, L 4.
Partisan Review, C 105.
Pastoral Life, C 39, D 12, D 42, L 28, R 40, R 41.
Pastoral Psychology, E 14, H 17.
Paulist Press, H 17, P 13, R 8, V 7.
Pediatrics, D 16.
Perspectives (Fides), D 40.
Pflaum, S 94.
Philosophy, G 19.
Philosophy Today, E 22.
Phylon, F 19.
Pilgrim Press, M 74.
Planned Parenthood, C 1, S 157.
Playboy, D 55, M 49.
Political Quarterly, H 33.
The Pope Speaks, B 54.
Population Council, P 55.
Population Studies, B 57.
Practitioner, P 15.
Praeger, G 15.
Prentice-Hall, B 25, B 35, D 25, R 55, V 1.
The Priest, D 41, U 7.
Princeton University Press, F 49.
Psychiatry, A 98.
Public Affairs Committee, P 40.
Public Health Reports, A 127, C 6.
Putnam, A 130, C 44, C 48, H 14.

Quadrangle Books, K 20, S 3.

Random House, B 21, D 23, S 74, T 27.
Reader's Digest, M 3, R 9.
Redbook, L 3.
Religious Education, F 26.
Renewal, M 73, M 87.
Report, R 11.

Rutgers Law Review, L 12.

Sacramentum Mundi, S 1.
Sage Publications, S 23.
St. Anthony's Messenger, C 102, M 20, M 21, O 26, S 19,
    V 6.
St Louis Post Dispatch, F 37.
St. Louis Review, B 67.
St. Martin's, H 62, S 126.
St. Paul Editions (Boston), C 30, C 63, H 71, P 13.
San Diego (Calif.) Evening Tribune, C 9.
San Francisco Public Library, S 164.
Saturday Review, H 2, W 43.
Saunders, M 48.
Scepter, D 2, H 63.
Science, C 28, D 9, D 37, H 39, M 11, R 12.
Science Digest, I 26.
Science News, E 12.
Scientific American, F 56, L 35, T 29.
Scribner, S 32.
Secker and Warburg, F 55.
Seminar, S 100.
Seventeen, C 4, G 28, M 55.
Sex Information and Education Council of the United States,
        S 64, S 65.  See also: D 42.
Sheed and Ward, C 16, C 118, D 45, E 30, H 76, M 10,
        M 62, O 28, S 20, S 92.
Sign, G 33, H 27, K 6, M 24.
Social Action, C 69.
Social Casework, B 8, C 47.
Social Forces, C 71.
Social Justice Review, B 3, C 33, F 21, F 42, I 2, J 5,
        M 79.
Social Problems, B 7, M 17.
Social Science Quarterly, P 68.
Sociological Abstracts, G 14.
Sociological Analysis, M 25, R 62.
Sociological Quarterly, M 66, U 14.
South Dakota Law Review, S 125.
Southern Medical Journal, W 7.
The Soviet Review, G 22.
Spartan House (Los Angeles, Calif.), D 46.
Standard Law Review, E 31.
Stein and Day, W 52.
Studies in Family Planning, J 6.
Suffolk University Law Review, A 86, U 1.
S.V.D. Publications, F 40.
Syracuse University Press, L 36.